General editor: Graham Handley

CW01661677

Brodie's Notes on William Shakespeare's

Measure for Measure

A. J. P. Smith BA(Oxon)
English Department, Kingswood School, Bath

Pan Books London and Sydney

First published 1985 by Pan Books Ltd
Cavaye Place, London SW10 9PG
9 8 7 6 5
© Pan Books Ltd 1985
ISBN 0 330 50201 8

Other titles by A. J. P. Smith in the Brodie's Notes series:
Henry IV Part 1
Richard II

Photoset by Parker Typesetting Service, Leicester
Printed and bound in Great Britain by
Richard Clay (The Chaucer Press) Ltd, Bungay, Suffolk

This book is sold subject to the condition that it shall not, by way of trade or otherwise, be lent, re-sold, hired out, or otherwise circulated without the publisher's prior consent in any form of binding or cover other than that in which it is published and without a similar condition including this condition being imposed on the subsequent purchaser

Contents

Preface

This student revision aid is based on the principle that in any close examination of Shakespeare's plays 'the text's the thing'. Seeing a performance, or listening to a tape or record of a performance, is essential and is in itself a valuable and stimulating experience in understanding and appreciation. However, a real evaluation of Shakespeare's greatness, of his universality and of the nature of his literary and dramatic art, can only be achieved by constant application to the texts of the plays themselves. These revised editions of Brodie's Notes are intended to supplement that process through detailed critical commentary.

The first aim of each book is to fix the whole play in the reader's mind by providing a concise summary of the plot, relating it back, where appropriate, to its source or sources. Subsequently the book provides a summary of each scene, followed by *critical comments*. These may convey its importance in the dramatic structure of the play, creation of atmosphere, indication of character development, significance of figurative language etc, and they will also explain or paraphrase difficult words or phrases and identify meaningful references. At the end of each act revision questions are set to test the student's specific and broad understanding and appreciation of the play.

An extended critical commentary follows this scene by scene analysis. This embraces such major elements as characterization, imagery, the use of blank verse and prose, soliloquies and other aspects of the play which the editor considers need close attention. The paramount aim is to send the reader back to the text. The book concludes with a series of revision questions which require a detailed knowledge of the play; the first of these has notes by the editor of what *might* be included in a written answer. The intention is to stimulate and to guide; the whole emphasis of this commentary is to encourage the student's *involvement* in the play, to develop disciplined critical responses and thus promote personal enrichment through the imaginative experience of our greatest writer.

Graham Handley

Line references in these Notes are to the *Arden Shakespeare: Measure for Measure*, but as references are also given to particular acts and scenes, the Notes may be used with any edition of the play.

Shakespeare and the Elizabethan Playhouse

William Shakespeare was born in Stratford-upon-Avon in 1564, and there are reasons to suppose that he came from a relatively prosperous family. He was probably educated at Stratford Grammar School and, at the age of eighteen, married Anne Hathaway, who was twenty-six. They had three children, a girl born shortly after their marriage, followed by twins in 1585 (the boy died in 1596). It seems likely that Shakespeare left for London shortly after a company of visiting players had visited Stratford in 1585, for by 1592 – according to the jealous testimony of one of his fellow-writers Robert Greene – he was certainly making his way both as actor and dramatist. The theatres were closed because of the plague in 1593; when they reopened Shakespeare worked with the Lord Chamberlain's men, later the King's men, and became a shareholder in each of the two theatres with which he was most closely associated, the Globe and the Blackfriars. He later purchased New Place, a considerable property in his home town of Stratford, to which he retired in 1611; there he entertained his great contemporary Ben Jonson (1572–1637) and the poet Michael Drayton (1563–1631). An astute businessman, Shakespeare lived comfortably in the town until his death in 1616.

This is a very brief outline of the life of our greatest writer, for little more can be said of him with certainty, though the plays – and poems – are living witness to the wisdom, humanity and many-faceted nature of the man. He was both popular and successful as a dramatist, perhaps less so as an actor. He probably began work as a dramatist in the late 1580s, by collaborating with other playwrights and adapting old plays, and by 1598 Francis Meres was paying tribute to his excellence in both comedy and tragedy. His first original play was probably *Love's Labour's Lost* (1590) and while the theatres were closed during the plague he wrote his narrative poems *Venus and Adonis* (1593) and *The Rape of Lucrece* (1594). The sonnets were almost certainly written in the 1590s though not published until 1609; the first 126 are addressed to a young man who was his friend and patron, while the rest are concerned with the 'dark lady'.

The dating of Shakespeare's plays has exercised scholars ever since the publication of the First Folio (1623), which listed them as comedies, histories and tragedies. It seems more important to look at them chronologically as far as possible, in order to trace Shakespeare's considerable development as a dramatist. The first period, say to the middle of the 1590s, included such plays as *Love's Labour's Lost, The Comedy of Errors, Richard III, The Taming of the Shrew, Romeo and Juliet* and *Richard II*. These early plays embrace the categories listed in the First Folio, so that Shakespeare the craftsman is evident in his capacity for variety of subject and treatment. The next phase includes *A Midsummer's Night's Dream, The Merchant of Venice, Henry IV Parts 1 and 2, Henry V* and *Much Ado About Nothing*, as well as *Julius Caesar, As You Like It* and *Twelfth Night*. These are followed, in the early years of the century, by his great tragic period: *Hamlet, Othello, King Lear* and *Macbeth*, with *Antony and Cleopatra* and *Coriolanus* belonging to 1607–09. The final phase embraces the romances (1610–13), *Cymbeline, The Tempest* and *The Winter's Tale* and the historical play *Henry VIII*.

Each of these revision aids will place the individual text under examination in the chronology of the remarkable dramatic output that spanned twenty years from the early 1590s to about 1613. The practical theatre for which Shakespeare wrote and acted derived from the inn courtyards in which performances had taken place, the few playhouses in his day being modelled on their structure. They were circular or hexagonal in shape, allowing from the balconies and boxes around the walls full view of the stage. This large stage, which had no scenery, jutted out into the pit, the most extensive part of the theatre, where the poorer people – the 'groundlings' – stood. There was no roof (though the Blackfriars, used from 1608 onwards, was an indoor theatre) and thus bad weather meant no performance. Certain plays were acted at court, and these private performances normally marked some special occasion. Costumes, often rich ones, were used, and music was a common feature, with musicians on or under the stage; this sometimes had additional features, for example a trapdoor to facilitate the entry of a ghost. Women were barred by law from appearing on stage, and all female parts were played by boy actors; this undoubtedly explains the many instances in Shakespeare where a woman has to conceal her identity by disguising

herself as a man, e.g. Rosalind in *As You Like It*, Viola in *Twelfth Night*.

Shakespeare and his contemporaries often adapted their plays from sources in history and literature, extending an incident or a myth or creating a dramatic narrative from known facts. They were always aware of their own audiences, and frequently included topical references, sometimes of a satirical flavour, which would appeal to – and be understood by – the groundlings as well as their wealthier patrons who occupied the boxes. Shakespeare obviously learned much from his fellow dramatists and actors, being on good terms with many of them. Ben Jonson paid generous tribute to him in the lines prefaced to the First Folio of Shakespeare's plays:

Thou art a monument without a tomb,
And art alive still, while thy book doth live
And we have wits to read, and praise to give.

Among his contemporaries were Thomas Kyd (1558–94) and Christopher Marlowe (1564–93). Kyd wrote *The Spanish Tragedy*, the revenge motif here foreshadowing the much more sophisticated treatment evident in *Hamlet*, while Marlowe evolved the 'mighty line' of blank verse, a combination of natural speech and elevated poetry. The quality and variety of Shakespeare's blank verse owes something to the innovatory brilliance of Marlowe but carries the stamp of individuality, richness of association, technical virtuosity and, above all, the genius of imaginative power.

The texts of Shakespeare's plays are still rich sources for scholars, and the editors of these revision aids have used the Arden editions of Shakespeare, which are regarded as pre-eminent for their scholarly approach. They are strongly recommended for advanced students, but other editions, like The New Penguin Shakespeare, The New Swan, The Signet are all good annotated editions currently available. A reading list of selected reliable works on the play being studied is provided at the end of each commentary and students are advised to turn to these as their interest in the play deepens.

Literary terms used in these notes

Blank verse Unrhymed verse in ten-syllable lines.
Climax The crucial moment, of high emotional charge – usually occurs just before the resolution of the drama.
Colloquial Words which are used in everyday speech.
Dénouement The moment in the play when the various complications of the plot are unravelled.
Diction The way in which a writer chooses his words.
Dramatic irony Occurs when a character in a play speaks words the true significance of which he does not understand. The audience, however, is assumed to be in possession of the significance of the character's utterance.
Imagery Figurative, rather than literal, language designed to enhance the reader's imaginative, sensory, intellectual response to what is being referred to. Often, more narrowly, applied to a work's similes and metaphors.
Irony Occurs when the surface meaning of a statement is the reverse of its underlying meaning.
Lyrical A highly emotional utterance, which usually betokens what is in a character's heart. Often the words have a melodious quality.
Metaphor A figure of speech in which a comparison is expressed or implied between two (often dissimilar) things, but without using 'like' or 'as'.
Pathos Occurs when a piece of writing evokes pity.
Personification Occurs when an inanimate object, or abstraction, is treated as though it were a person.
Pun A play on words that sound, or are spelt, the same but have different meanings.
Rhetorical Language which is deliberately contrived so as to be particularly persuasive or emotive. Often associated with a prepared, publicly-delivered speech.
Rhythm Language as it is spoken, has a naturally distributed sound-emphasis. When these emphases (or 'stresses') occur with some pattern, it is called 'metre'.
Simile A comparison introduced by 'like' or 'as'.
Soliloquy The name given to a character's speech, when, alone on the stage, he speaks his innermost thoughts and feelings directly to the audience.
Sub-plot That part of the story which is separate from the main sequence of the narrative.
Symbolism Occurs when an object has the power to arouse particular thoughts and feelings in an audience. Sometimes an episode in a play possesses this power. An object, or event, may give 'concrete' form to an abtract idea.

The play
Plot, sources and treatment, date

Plot

Vienna is in a state of moral decay owing to the leniency of Duke Vincentio. In order to rectify matters, the Duke decides to absent himself from the city, leaving its affairs in the hands of Angelo, who has a reputation for virtue and moral strictness. In fact, the Duke does not intend to desert Vienna: his plan is to return disguised as a 'friar', so that he may keep a watchful eye on Angelo and his management of the Deputyship.

Once in control, Angelo, true to form, embarks upon a campaign to rid the city of immorality. His instrument for so doing is the law, and he re-invokes a disused statute which demands the death penalty for the sin of fornication. Angelo also demolishes the brothels in the suburbs of Vienna, to the outrage of Mistress Overdone and the bawd, Pompey. Claudio is the first victim of the anti-fornication legislation. To everyone's dismay, it is soon apparent that Angelo does not intend to exercise mercy. Claudio asks Lucio to enquire of his sister (Isabella), who is about to enter a nunnery, if she will plead his cause before Angelo. Lucio complies, and reluctantly Isabella agrees to go to the Deputy and seek a reprieve for her brother.

Isabella is at first unsuccessful in wringing mercy from Angelo, and he refutes her pleas. But he asks that she return the next day to plead her cause once more. By this time it is apparent that Angelo lusts after the virginal Isabella. In the meantime, the Duke has returned to the city, in his 'Friar' guise, and he is told, by the Provost, of the fate of Claudio and Juliet. Juliet carries Claudio's unborn child and she receives comfort from the 'Friar'.

At her second meeting with Angelo, Isabella renews her plea for her brother's life. Again she is apparently unsuccessful. Eventually, however, after some evasive hinting at his desires, Angelo declares his passion for her and offers to spare Claudio, if she will surrender to his lust. Horrified, Isabella spurns his contemptible offer. She goes to Claudio, to acquaint him with Angelo's proposal, and to prepare him to face his execution.

The 'Friar' has already arrived at Claudio's prison cell and administered words of comfort. Claudio appears reconciled. A few moments later, however, Isabella tells him of Angelo's offer to her; at first, he shares her disgust at the proposal, but as the awful prospect of his death dawns upon him, together with the salvation which is possible if Isabella surrenders, the young man finds that he can maintain his equanimity no longer: he bursts into an impassioned plea that Isabella should save him – even at the expense of her chastity. Isabella is appalled at her brother's 'weakness' and denounces his 'cowardice'. Claudio is duly mortified at his lapse and becomes resigned once more to his death.

The 'Friar', however, has overheard this conversation. After Claudio has withdrawn, the 'Friar' proposes a possible solution to Isabella's cruel dilemma. Angelo, like Claudio, once contracted a clandestine marriage to a girl named Mariana. Subsequently, he deserted her. Isabella is instructed that she should appear to accept Angelo's foul proposal, but she must get his agreement to meet him in a dark and secluded place. Mariana must keep this assignation in Isabella's place. The 'Friar' believes that once Angelo is confronted with the fact that he has consummated his marriage, he will be forced to acknowledge its existence. Also, Isabella will be saved from shame, and Mariana, because she still loves Angelo, will be 'advantaged'. Claudio, of course, in the meantime, will have been reprieved.

All goes according to plan: Mariana, the substitute-Isabella, meets Angelo. Unfortunately, however, the dastardly Deputy, despite, as he believes, having had his way with Isabella, does not keep his side of the bargain, and he orders that the execution of Claudio should proceed, and that Claudio's head should arrive before him by five o'clock in the afternoon. Hastily, the 'Friar' arranges for the head of Ragozine, a pirate who has died of a fever, to be sent to Angelo. The substitution will not be realized because of the facial similarity between Claudio and Ragozine! Isabella is not told of this trick and is led to believe that her brother has been executed. However, she is advised by the 'Friar' that the Duke's return is imminent and that she should appeal to him for justice.

On the arrival of the Duke, Isabella publicly denounces Angelo and reveals his sins. Mariana also reveals what happened between her and Angelo and claims that he is her husband. Naturally, Angelo denies these 'stories', pronouncing them to be malicious slanders. The Duke also affects not to believe the two women, and he departs, instructing Angelo to enquire further into the matter. A mysterious friar is thought to have had a hand in the 'slanders', and he is summoned to give evidence.

The Duke returns, wearing once again his Friar's habit. In his disguise, the Duke denies having inspired the two women to slander Angelo, but he tells the assembled company that he has been a 'looker-on', who has observed the profound corruption which has gripped Vienna whilst the Duke was absent. His words inspire an attack upon his person, and in the ensuing scuffle Lucio removes the friar's hood. The Duke stands revealed.

Angelo now realizes that he can no longer maintain his innocence: he confesses and begs to be put to death. The Duke tells him that he must first marry Mariana – a genuine friar is conveniently standing-by to conduct the ceremony. The newly-married Angelo is then condemned to death. Before matters can proceed, Mariana falls to her knees and begs for her husband's life. Isabella, despite her belief that Claudio is dead, is requested tearfully by Mariana to add her voice to the plea for Angelo. Isabella complies and falls to her knees before the Duke. At this point, the Duke reveals that Claudio has been saved from execution. Brother and sister are reunited. Claudio and Angelo are pardoned for their respective offences and the Duke proposes marriage to Isabella. Lucio, who has been a thorn in the Duke's flesh during the course of the action – constantly slandering him – is at first condemned to be whipped and then hanged. But at the last minute the Duke relents and orders Lucio to marry the whore who has borne his child. Lucio protests that this is a worse punishment than being whipped and hanged. The Duke hints once more that Isabella should marry him, but she remains silent about the matter.

Sources and treatment

Shakespeare derived his plot principally from two sources: a story in Cinthio's *Hecatommithi* and George Whetstone's drama, *Promos and Cassandra*. Both sources tell of a corrupt deputy, who strikes an unholy bargain with a virtuous maiden, involving the surrender of her virginity in return for the reprieve of a convicted brother. In both versions the virgin yields, only to have the deputy go back on his word and have the brother executed; the body of the dead man is sent to the heroine. In Cinthio's version the brother is actually killed, whereas Whetstone has the brother saved by a jailor and a substitute body is sent to the sister. Cinthio and Whetstone have the heroine seek redress from higher authority and conclude with her marrying her former persecutor. In Whetstone, the brother is revealed to be still alive.

From this brief outline it will be apparent that Shakespeare altered the plots of his sources; he differs from Cinthio in that Isabella does not actually make love with the deputy, Claudio's life is saved and, of course, Isabella does not marry Angelo. Shakespeare incorporates from Whetstone the notion that Claudio is saved by means of a substitution-trick.

In handling these sources Shakespeare made the following important changes:

1 Isabella is made a novitiate nun. This adds dramatic intensity to her reaction to Angelo's proposal and ensures that she has a valid reason for not consenting to it: she would have been guilty of a mortal sin, and had Claudio allowed himself to have been saved by such a means, he too would have been damned.

2 Mariana is invented. The coincidence that Angelo had contracted to marry her links him with the sin of Claudio, who is to be executed. When Angelo makes love to Mariana, he too commits fornication. Angelo is shown to be more heinous in that he deserted his former love, whereas Claudio expected to marry Juliet.

Thus Mariana enables Isabella's honour to be saved, renders Isabella's plea for Angelo's life more acceptable, and ensures that Shakespeare has a fitting mate for Angelo. It is obviously entirely unconvincing that Cinthio and Whetstone have Isabella marrying the man who has violated her; Shakespeare neatly avoids this improbability.

3 Angelo is made into an interesting character in that he is a severe, puritanical man, rather than a simple villain.

4 Shakespeare, in making the Duke a disguised ruler who returns, greatly increases his importance in the story. He can now be seen as a reconciling, guiding force, who embodies in his person the Christian spirit of forgiveness and leads Isabella to an understanding of the value of Christian charity. It is surely not coincidental that the Duke returns to Vienna in the guise of a friar.

5 In Cinthio the brother is convicted of rape; in Whetstone it is rape again, but the girl consented. Shakespeare softens Claudio's crime by inventing the clandestine marriage – he thus becomes a suitable candidate for mercy, and Angelo's harshness in not granting it is emphasized.

Date

The first recorded performance of *Measure for Measure* was on 26 December 1604. It was presented at the court of James I. It seems reasonable to suppose that Shakespeare wrote the play earlier in the same year. It had probably been performed at the Globe prior to its performance at court, but no record of these productions exists. The first printed version of the play is to be found in the First Folio (1623).

Measure for Measure – a 'Problem Play'

Measure for Measure may be designated a 'Problem Play' for two reasons.

1 There is the 'problem' of classification. Elements in the story clearly belong to the fairy-story genre – the returning Duke whom nobody recognizes; Angelo does not recognize Mariana, although they make love; Ragozine passes for Claudio; marriages are proposed in the dénouement which appear to have little chance of success, yet we are asked to rejoice at them. Such 'unrealistic' elements, whilst acceptable in the realm of comedy, jar against the strongly 'realistic' elements which are apparent in the first half of the play – in particular, the convincingly-explored and potentially tragic relationship between Angelo, Isabella and Claudio, where dark forces are at work. Evil, of course, is present in the Comedies, but we are not asked to take it seriously, and its practitioners tend to be 'stage-villains'. This is not true of *Measure for Measure*: in the first part of the play Angelo is altogether a more substantial and vividly-realized character. In *Measure for Measure*, Shakespeare has his characters undergo sudden conversions and perpetrate 'tricks' which bring about the happy ending but which do not sit easily with the tragic potentialities of Acts I and II of the play.

2 *Measure for Measure* is a 'Problem Play' in the sense that it poses the audience certain moral/ethical problems. We are asked to make judgements: should Isabella have 'given in' to Angelo and saved her brother? Is chastity to be valued above charity? What is the role of the ruler? How is authority best exerted? What is the role of law in sexual matters? What is the place of mercy in the exercise of justice? Should Angelo have been pardoned? Was Isabella justified in conniving at the Mariana-substitution? Does the means (disguise and deception) justify the end (harmony and happiness)? Why does Isabella not reply to the Duke's offer of marriage? We are invited to arrive at judgements; Shakespeare, as always, is reticent when it comes to supplying clear-cut answers.

Scene summaries, critical commentaries, textual notes and revision questions

Act I Scene 1

Duke Vincentio informs Escalus, one of his oldest and most-valued counsellors, that he is going to hand over the government of Vienna to Angelo, whilst he absents himself from the city. Escalus is to be second-in-command. Angelo arrives and is also informed of the Duke's decision. After some initial qualms about his fitness for the post, Angelo agrees to accept absolute power in Vienna. The Duke clearly believes that it is Angelo's duty to do so, and that he is admirably equipped to govern. After expressing his confidence in the arrangement, Vincentio makes off speedily; Angelo bids him farewell and withdraws, with Escalus, to discuss matters of power with him.

Commentary

The Duke's opening speech introduces the theme of 'the properties of government' which is to occupy much of the play. Also, when Angelo is appointed Deputy, he is given absolute powers – in particular the power 'of mortality and mercy'. The theme of justice is obviously central to the drama which is about to unfold. The scene focuses on Angelo: he is called upon to put his virtues to the test; also he is instructed to 'enforce and qualify the laws'. We shall shortly see that he is strong on enforcement, but not so interested in qualification (i.e. mercy) which should accompany justice.

Angelo's request that some further test be made of his 'metal' before he is granted such powers, perhaps hints at some inner uncertainty. But the Duke's confidence, which is based upon Angelo's 'ample grace and honour', is not subject to doubt. In any case, Vincentio's contention is that Angelo should not be content to hide his light under a bushel – his virtue needs to be put to the test. The suggestion underlying this is that there may be something self-regarding about Angelo. The Duke's suggestion that he should use such gifts as nature has given him, turns out to be ironical: Angelo proves himself to be susceptible to the promptings of a rather different nature than the one that Vincentio has in mind!

The Duke's leave-taking is clearly hasty, and no reason is

given, as yet, for his departure. His dislike of public ostentation is sometimes thought to parallel the feelings of James I. Nonetheless, the scene is essentially formal and the verse is appropriately dignified, dealing with grand generalizations appropriate to the handing over of power.

properties Constituents.
affect (Speak) pretentiously.
put to know Forced to acknowledge.
science Knowledge.
lists Limits.
sufficiency Ability.
pregnant in i.e. in full command of.
warp Deviate from.
figure i.e. 'how well will he fulfil my role?'
soul i.e. with all my faculties of heart and intellect.
terror An appropriate emotion for a ruler to excite in his subjects.
character Quality.
thy belongings i.e. the qualities of character which Angelo possesses.
thine . . . proper Are not so absolutely your own property. The Duke is suggesting to Angelo that his manifest gifts should be employed for the public good, rather than in his private interests.
we had them not i.e. it would be wrong to hide our lights under bushels.
touch'd Tuned.
nature i.e. Nature requires that the gifts she gives us should manifest her own glory. We should give her thanks and use the gifts she bestows.
scruple Particle.
bend my speech Intend my words should be addressed to.
my part . . . advertise i.e. my function (as ruler) can be made manifest in him (Angelo).
remove Absence.
at full ourself i.e. possess my powers in full.
Mortality The power to exercise the death penalty.
first in question First came into consideration.
metal A pun. 'Mettle' meaning spirit, and it also refers back to the Duke's use of 'figure' (the Duke's face, stamped on a coin). Angelo suggests that the Duke should make some further test of his true worth (i.e. the 'metal' of his coinage).
leaven'd i.e. the choice was performed after careful consideration.
condition Subject to such urgent necessity.
prefers itself Has priority over all other considerations.
concernings That which concerns me.
importune Urge.
privily Secretly.
Aves Hails, acclamations.

safe discretion Sound judgement.
free Frank.
the bottom of my place The full nature of my official position.

Act I Scene 2

The scene opens with Lucio and friends discussing political matters. Obviously, they believe that the Duke's departure is connected with some secret diplomacy. Their talk shifts to bawdy subjects. They are interrupted by the arrival of Mistress Overdone, who brings the news that Claudio has been hailed off to prison and that he is shortly to be executed, the crime being fornication with Juliet. Pompey, tapster and general factotum to Mrs Overdone, enters with the news that Angelo has determined on the immediate destruction of all the brothels in the suburbs of Vienna. Mrs Overdone is not pleased. Clearly, Angelo is embarking upon a campaign to purge the city of immorality.

We next meet Claudio who, in the company of various officers, under the supervision of the Provost, is being led off to imprisonment. Juliet is also in attendance – she is with child. Claudio remarks that Angelo has re-enacted various statutes and penalties, which had long fallen into neglect under Vincentio's regime. Tyranny is in the offing; that Angelo is being unduly rigorous would seem to be the general feeling. We also learn that Claudio had contracted a clandestine marriage to Juliet, and, although this does not have the blessing of the Church, nonetheless they may be regarded as legally married.

In desperation, Claudio asks his friend Lucio to go to his sister, Isabella, who is about to enter a nunnery: perhaps she may be persuaded to go before Angelo and plead for her brother's life. This, at least, is Claudio's one remaining hope: he trusts that Angelo will be moved by Isabella's pleas for clemency.

Commentary

After the dignity of the opening scene, the picture of Viennese society which is presented here comes as something of a rude shock. Much of the talk between Lucio and the Gentleman concerns the subject of venereal disease, and, although the tone is light-hearted, we cannot escape the conclusion that there is something rotten in the city which Vincentio has recently left. The news that Angelo has ordered the demolition of all the brothels in the suburbs, indicates that the Deputy is prepared to undertake the drastic measures which are necessary to clean up the city. As Mistress Overdone comments: 'Here's a change indeed in the commonwealth.' Lucio is expecting to meet Claudio, but he has been carted off to prison for getting Juliet 'with child' – and he is threatened with the death penalty: Angelo has re-instituted some ancient statutes which have long been dormant under the rule of Vincentio.

When Claudio arrives, under arrest, it is apparent that he is, in fact, married to the girl whom he has seduced. There is some ambiguity here: Juliet is Claudio's wife in so far as they have undertaken a mutual exchange of vows – and this has the force of legality, but their marriage has not enjoyed the sanction of the Church. Technically, therefore, they have committed fornication. Essentially, the stance of the Church towards clandestine marriages was a double one: whilst it recognized their legality, they were at one and the same time, declared sinful – and the couple who indulged in such a marriage were required to obtain the blessing of the Church or stand condemned if they consummated their relationship. All this is rather confusing to modern ears, but the effect is to present Claudio as a man who has offended, yet to mitigate the severity of his offence. Thus, in adopting a rigorous attitude towards Claudio's 'crime', Angelo is portrayed as harsh and legalistic. Application of the law is not being tempered by mercy. It may be noted, in passing, that Juliet is also under arrest for the offence.

composition Agreement.
sanctimonious Pious. An allusion to the pirate who took the Ten Commandments as his figurehead – and obeyed them all, save one: 'Thou shalt not steal'!
functions Natural actions.
despite . . . grace Grace is used in two main senses: (a) Divine Mercy, and (b) the 'grace' which is said at meal-times.
pair of shears i.e. they are both the same, cut from the same piece of cloth.
lists . . . velvet Selvage (from which borders were made in garments) and the fine 'velvet' from which the garment itself was made. Lucio implies that he is superior to the Gentleman.
three-piled piece i.e. a pile of three thicknesses.
kersey Plain cloth.
pilled Bald. A reference to the effects of Mercury, commonly used as a treatment for venereal disease.
feelingly To the point.
drink after thee i.e. not from the same cup, for fear of catching venereal disease.

Mitigation Traditionally the bawd 'mitigates' the sexual desires of her clients!
dolours A pun on dolours meaning 'dollars' (i.e. he has spent a great deal of money under her roof), and dolours meaning 'sorrows' (the result of frequently contracting venereal disease).
A French Crown Yet another pun involving money, and the name for venereal disease. Cf. the earlier reference to baldness.
figuring Another monetary pun. The monarch's head was figured (engraved) on a coin.
sound Healthy.
the sweat Fever, associated with the plague – rife in London during Shakespeare's time.
Groping . . . river i.e. deceiving an innocent young girl.
plucked down Demolished.
service Pompey implies that brothel-keeping is a public service, with Mistress Overdone acting as a sort of blind Cupid – who brings 'lovers' together.
Thomas A traditional nickname for tapsters.
Provost It was his duty to oversee executions.
demi-god Semi-divine.
The words of heaven An obscure reference which probably means that Authority uses the words of heaven (i.e. Scripture) to add weight to mercy, sentence and punishment. It is sometimes taken as a direct allusion to Romans, 9, 15: 'I will have mercie on him, to whom I will shew mercie.'
ravin Ravenously devour.
bane Poison.
foppery Foolishness.
morality Moral teaching.
look'd after Regarded so closely.
fast my wife Although the marriage has not been solemnized in church, it has legal validity because the couple exchanged mutual vows.
denunciation Public proclamation.
outward order i.e. as demanded by the Church.
propagation Augmentation.
dower . . . for us They awaited such time as it took for a dowry to be raised by the friends of Juliet. Presumably, she was an orphan.
too gross Aspersions were cast upon her character: she is now with child.
glimpse of newness . . . Because of his newness in office, Angelo's perception of his role is faulty.
in his place i.e. it is of the nature (place) of tyranny.
eminence Self-importance.
stagger Hesitate (to say).
unscour'd i.e. fallen into disuse.
nineteen zodiacs Nineteen years.
worn Put into effect (refers to the 'penalties').

tickle Insecurely.
approbation Novitiate.
prone and speechless i.e. Isabella will be able to move Angelo, without any need to do anything (implied: 'stir from a prone position' and 'speak').
imposition Accusation.

Act I Scene 3

The Duke has not left Vienna. In conversation with Friar Thomas, he reveals his intentions: Angelo is to be used to enforce moral order on a society that has become corrupt because of the Duke's laxity. Vincentio intends to return to the city, disguised as a Friar – in this way he will be able to observe how Angelo fulfils his responsibilities.

Commentary

The Duke assumes his disguise as Friar Lodowick. It was a convention of the theatre of Shakespeare's day that a relatively minor change in a character's outward appearance rendered that character unrecognizable.

Vincentio's motives for leaving Vienna so hastily are now revealed: Angelo has been granted the Duke's authority to enforce the laws which the Duke himself has not seen fit to enforce on his own account. We may question here the validity of the Duke's position – it would seem that he is willing to palm off his responsibilities. However, given the necessity for the restoration of order in Vienna, his argument that it would be tyrannous of him to strike out against lawbreakers, who have been encouraged by his own permissive attitudes, has a degree of coherence which we are not invited to question. In any case, in assuming his disguise and returning to Vienna, the Duke is seen not to be giving up his responsibilities. We can take confidence from his presiding presence, that, such things as threaten to go wrong, may ultimately be righted when Vincentio decides to reveal himself!

The Duke also gives us insight into Angelo. The word 'precise' is often associated with rigid puritanism. Of course, such an attitude became a by-word for hypocrisy. Vincentio's closing remarks strongly suggest that Angelo is on trial. Questions are raised: will power corrupt? Are the outward actions of Angelo at one with his inward self?

Vincentio's statement that he is immune to 'the dribbling dart of love' is ironical in the light of his proposal to Isabella in the final scene, and suggests that his return to Vienna will involve a degree of self-exploration.

cost Expensive showiness.
bravery Display.
stricture Abstemiousness.
biting . . . bits . . . curbs The imagery here suggests restraining an unruly steed.
fourteen Nineteen years, according to Angelo.
fond Foolish.
to themselves are dead i.e. in effect, might as well be dead.
gall To hurt, to injure.
for . . . punishment The Duke says that by not enforcing the laws, and allowing permissiveness to run riot, he virtually connived at lawlessness.
Who may . . . slander Angelo is to impose order, using the authority of the Duke, but the Duke himself will remain apart from this process, lest justice (which he admits he has not enforced) should fall into disrepute.
habit i.e. the garments of a friar.
precise Scrupulously moral, puritanical.
Envy Malice.
scarce . . . flows i.e. is the least passionate of men.
appetite Physical needs.
power . . . be Perhaps the Duke suspects that power will corrupt Angelo.

Act I Scene 4

Isabella, a novice, laments that the Poor Clares (one of the strictest orders) is not restrictive enough for her tastes. The arrival of Lucio causes some agitation to Isabella's companion: 'It is a man's voice!'

Lucio tells Isabella of her brother's plight, but, at first, she thinks that he is lying when he tells her that he has got a woman 'with child'. After hearing of the unfortunate girl's name, details of the Duke's sudden departure and Angelo's government, Isabella agrees to intercede for Claudio's life. Modestly, she doubts her powers of persuasion.

Commentary

The action is in a nunnery. Isabella has decided upon withdrawal from the world. The ideals of the convent stand starkly opposed to those of the world and sexuality which we have encountered hitherto. Lucio arrives, bringing with him the news of the Duke's departure and the condemnation of Claudio. Isabella, the contemplative, is thus forced to make a choice between withdrawal and involvement in the world. She chooses to plead for Claudio's life, although, ironically, we may suppose that her view of morality would lead her to sympathize more with Angelo than her brother. There is an obvious parallel between Angelo and Isabella: both, by force of circumstances, have been placed in a position whereby they must abandon formerly held notions of keeping themselves aloof from the world. When they meet, the issues are to be presented even more starkly: Angelo confronts the sensuality in his nature, and Isabella finds herself pleading for her brother's life – although she condemns the sin of which he stands accused. The events of the play force Angelo and Isabella to recognize the inadequacy of formerly-held beliefs and to surrender that proud part of themselves which they, at this stage, believe sets them apart from the common run of humanity.

votarists of Saint Clare Members of the order of nuns known as Poor Clares.
unsworn Yet to take her final vows.
stead me Grant me the service.
Not . . . you Not to prolong matters.
make . . . story Stop playing the fool with me.
lapwing A bird which feigns injury to lure predators from its young. Hence, 'dissembler'.
enskied Heavenly.
seedness Sowing-time.
foison Plenty.
tilth Tillage.
Bore . . . hand Deceived.
nerves of state The political ins-and-outs.
giving out Published intentions.
with full line In complete freedom (by the Duke's authority).
snow-broth Melted snow.
wanton stings Unrestrained urgings of desire.
sense i.e. the senses.
rebate Dulls (the edge of).
run by Passed by; i.e. freedom and licence have escaped legal restraint.
heavy sense Serious consequence.
pith of business Essentials of my business.
censur'd Sentenced.
owe Own.

Revision questions on Act I

1 Show how our understanding of the character of Angelo has developed during the first act.

2 What picture of life in Vienna is presented in Act I?

3 What reasons does the Duke give for absenting himself from Vienna?

4 Whom do you consider the most sympathetic character in the play so far? Give reasons for your answer.

5 Write a critical analysis of the character of Isabella and her attitude to life.

Act II Scene 1

A courtroom. Angelo announces his determination to enforce the law with unremitting vigour. Escalus, pleading for the life of Claudio, tells of the hapless young man's good family and urges that the law should not be enforced as a blunt instrument; daringly, he suggests that Angelo himself might have fallen from grace had a similar opportunity presented itself. Loftily, Angelo retorts that it is one thing to be tempted, but quite another thing to fall; he also refutes the argument that fallible men have no right to judge the fallibility of their fellow men. The Provost is ordered to make preparations for Claudio's execution.

Elbow, an incompetent officer, next enters to present the case against Pompey, who is accused of attempting to lure the wife of the idiotic Froth into prostitution. The foolishness of Elbow and the comic interventions of Pompey soon prove tedious to Angelo, who leaves the courtroom. Escalus remains to hear the case. No progress is made and the proceedings come to an end with Escalus ordering Pompey not to appear before the court again, on pain of being whipped. Escalus tells Elbow to augment the Watch with six or seven more officers and then departs with a Justice (silent until now) lamenting the fate which awaits Claudio on the morrow.

Commentary

The opening speech of Escalus in which he pleads for leniency towards Claudio establishes further sympathy for the young man's plight: if such a self-evidently wise counsellor thinks that

Angelo's approach is too harsh, then there must be something in his argument. But Escalus goes further and points out to Angelo that had a different set of circumstances arisen, then Angelo himself might find himself condemned. Ironical, indeed, in the light of the imminent arrival of Isabella. Angelo's reply is to underline, self-righteously, that it is 'one thing to be tempted,/Another thing to fall'. Again the Deputy will shortly find himself condemned by the standards that he sets for himself. Interestingly, Angelo does not deny the possibility of his being tempted: beneath the icy exterior there may lurk a more passionate nature. Even so, Angelo refuses to countenance the argument of Escalus: the fact that he might possess similar faults, in no way extenuates the fault of Claudio – the law must be above such partiality. Such absolutism is characteristic of Angelo's attitude towards his governorship. At this stage, when matters can be still thought of impersonally, Angelo is prepared to acknowledge that he himself is not above the law – should he commit an offence, then his punishment should be commensurate with the crime. It is left to the Provost to comment that justice, in the case of Claudio has, in fact, not been humanely administered, although he does not question the legality of the proceedings.

The arrival of Froth, Elbow and Pompey immediately lightens the tone and prevents it slipping into tragedy. The issue here is human sexuality versus the law – just as it was with Claudio. The area of debate here is significant – the law has always found it 'difficult': legislation which seeks to control this most wayward and basic of human drives must always encounter formidable problems. This is not to argue that the law has no place in such matters, but Shakespeare clearly indicates that when it comes to grappling with the human world, the ruthless legalism of Angelo cannot operate satisfactorily. As the meanderings of Elbow, and the obfuscations of Pompey become more and more absurd, so the rigid Angelo becomes more and more uneasy and exasperated. Eventually, he stalks out, leaving the investigation of the case to the good-humoured patience of Escalus: 'Which is the wiser here, justice or iniquity?' – a good question! One thing is certain, the outrageous pragmatism of Pompey is diametrically opposed to the formalism of Angelo. In setting free the malefactors, it is arguable that Escalus adopts the sensible approach towards fallible human nature; equally we might say that his leniency is reminiscent of the ideas which typified the *laissez-faire* Duke's reign.

custom Familiarity.
cut a little . . . death Escalus asks that the law should be used with discrimination: as a sharp knife, to cut away wrongdoing with delicacy, rather than a blunt axe – hacking down all and sundry.
affections Desires, lusts.
acting . . . blood The acting out of your physical desires.
What knows . . . thieves The law cannot take account of the fact that thieves may be called upon to pass judgement on thieves.
pregnant Apparent.
censure Sentence.
pattern out Act as a pattern for.
nothing . . . partial i.e. I do not look for judgement to be partial when I die.
run . . . none A difficult passage. The implication would seem to be that Vincentio has run away from the difficulties of governing ('brakes of ice') and that he has therefore not made himself answerable for the problems of state.
common houses Whorehouses.
benefactors i.e. malefactors. One of Elbow's many malapropisms – misuses of words.
out at elbow i.e. pitifully lacking in wit.
parcel bawd Part-time bawd.
professes i.e. it is her profession.
hot-house Bath-house. Often a 'cover' for a whorehouse.
detest i.e. protest.
cardinally i.e. carnally.
means i.e. by means of her pimp.
honourable Sarcastic, of course.
misplaces i.e. misuses words.
stewed prunes Euphemistic term for prostitutes.
the thing . . . of i.e. venereal disease. 'wot'=know.
Allhallond Eve Allhallows Eve.
open room Public room.
respected i.e. suspected.
Justice or Iniquity Morality Play characters of great stupidity.
Hannibal Cannibal.
courses Way of life.
colour Conceal.
splay Sterilize.
drabs 'Tarts'.
knaves Rascals.
heading Beheading.
bay The part of a house which is beneath a gable.
carman Carter.
jade Broken-down horse.
sufficient Capable.
that oft looks so What appears as mercy, may not in fact be merciful.

Pardon . . . woe To pardon a wrongdoer is often to encourage a second offence.

Act II Scene 2

The Provost adds his voice to those who would plead for Claudio's life and goes so far as to remind Angelo that it has been known for judges to feel that they have imposed a death sentence unwisely – after the victim has been executed. But Angelo remains intransigent and orders the Provost to find a fit place to dispose of Juliet, who is nearing the moment when she must give birth.

Isabella is admitted to the governor's presence. Whilst not condoning Claudio's action, Isabella nonetheless asks that her brother should be pardoned. Angelo refuses, pointing out that to condemn the sin but not the perpetrator is manifestly to undermine the status of the law. Isabella begs that mercy should be shown – it is not too late. Angelo retorts that, as far as he is concerned, it is too late: the law must be upheld, and it would be unfair to show partiality in this case. Elaborating upon the reasons why Angelo should be merciful, Isabella reminds him that her brother is not ready to die and that human beings should be on their guard, lest the faults which they condemn reside in the bosoms of those who do the condemning. Lucio, who has been interjecting occasional encouragement to Isabella, feels that Angelo is moved by this argument, which seems to question the very basis upon which one man in authority may judge another. By this time it has become clear that Angelo is sexually attracted to Isabella, and our suspicions are confirmed when he asks that Isabella should return 'tomorrow'.

Angelo ends the scene castigating himself for desiring the manifestly virtuous Isabella. He feels a great deal of self-disgust.

Commentary

The good-hearted Provost's plea that Angelo should show mercy represents the voice of common decency. Angelo is adamant. The cold-hearted 'disposal' of Juliet, who is on the point of giving birth, places Angelo firmly amongst the forces which are 'anti-life' – to him she is a mere 'fornicatress'.

Isabella's opening remarks to Angelo reveal the difficulty of her position. She seems uneasy in so far as she finds herself asking that the fault be condemned but not the wrong-doer.

Angelo easily dismisses such special pleading; Lucio finds her approach 'too cold'. Isabella's next tack is to speak of the mercy which 'becomes' the ruler, and this leads to her questioning of the very right of one man to judge another. In this she reiterates the notion put forward by Escalus in an earlier scene: if Angelo had 'slipped' then he would have the right to expect mercy. She goes so far as to suggest that had the roles been reversed, then Claudio would have shown mercy to Angelo. She next puts forward the argument of Divine Mercy: God shows mercy to mankind, and the quality when exercised by men reveals them in a God-like aspect. The climax of her plea comes when she questions the notion of authority. It is here that we reach one of the central 'problems' of the play. To Isabella a man 'dress'd in a little brief authority' cuts a ridiculous, even a bestial figure. We may agree with her. Yet we must also recognize that it is the duty of the ruler to rule (indeed, this is a God-given responsibility). In the course of ruling, of necessity, 'authority' must see that the laws are kept. Here the case of Claudio becomes relevant. 'Authority' has exercised the right to judge and sentence him to death – but such blind enforcement is self-evidently 'most ignorant'. Claudio may have broken the rules by consummating his marriage before the Church had given its sanction, but the punishment is way out of proportion to the misdemeanour. Claudio should have his 'knuckles rapped', perhaps, but the death sentence, whilst 'legal', shows a profound lack of judgement. The prerogative of the ruler, mercy, should have been exercised. It is somewhat ironic that the hardened exploiter of women (Pompey) gets away with a caution.

By the time that Isabella has reached the climax of her plea, another factor has become apparent: Angelo lusts after her. The judge himself is shown to be a prey to sin – indeed, he is subject to the very vice which he has been so busily rooting out in others. In a sense, remarks made by Escalus and Isabella have prepared us for this moment. For the first time in the play Angelo becomes human: as he speaks of his feelings at the end of the scene, we see a man racked by conflicting desires. The certitudes have evaporated; he is tortured by guilt. Ironically, it is Isabella's manifest saintliness as well as her beauty that has entrapped him – and he hates himself for it. To survive from now on he must lead a double life: his appearance of virtue belies his underlying lustfulness.

in a dream i.e. not in reality.
judgment . . . doom i.e. judges have felt sorry about the sentences they

have imposed – too late, for the victims have already been executed.
mine My affair.
shall well be spar'd I shall be well rid of you.
groaning i.e. in childbirth.
will and will not Isabella wishes to plead for mercy and yet acknowledges that she abhors the 'crime'.
let it be his fault . . . brother Let the fault be condemned but not my brother.
every . . . done i.e. faults, in themselves, are obviously to be condemned before they are committed.
cipher . . . actor Angelo says that it is a necessary attribute of a judge to punish offenders, rather than merely condemn them: to fail to do so, would be to deny the function of a judge and render himself a mere cipher.
I had a brother Isabella gives up the struggle.
longs Belongs.
deputed Refers to judges who hold their power by virtue of the king's appointment.
slipp'd Erred.
potency Power.
vein i.e. the best way to touch his heart.
top of judgement i.e. God Himself.
gross selves i.e. that part of ourselves which feeds us.
it hath slept Angelo condemns earlier leniency, which has encouraged vice.
glass A magic crystal. A 'crystal ball'.
new, . . . conceiv'd The distinction is between wickedness, which is conceived of in these present times, and wickedness which might come to be perpetrated if the law turns a blind eye.
gall Cause to suffer.
pelting Trivial.
oak . . . myrtle Heaven directs its attention to objects of Divine Wrath and it is merciful towards the lesser sinners.
glassy Man's essence (soul) as seen in a mirror.
spleens i.e. the spleen was traditionally the organ of the body from which laughter originated.
mortal They would laugh themselves to death, or into the human condition.
weigh . . . ourself Isabella says that she cannot judge her brother (i.e. her fellow men) by the standards which she might apply to herself.
Art avis'd o' that? Have you learned that lesson?
put Attribute.
medicine Healing property.
skins . . . th' top i.e. covers over the surface of the wound without healing it. Thus those who have authority are able to conceal their own follies.
sense . . . sense breeds with it She has spoken such good sense that the sensual part of myself is encouraged by what she has said. Ironically,

Angelo finds himself sexually aroused by Isabella's icy reasoning.
heaven Isabella is thinking of divine rewards; Angelo, doubtless would be thinking of a more earthly reward to be obtained from her!
fond sickles Shekels (money) so foolishly prized by the world.
tested Refined, pure.
preserved souls i.e. nuns' souls, preserved from the taint of evil.
temporal Worldly.
prayer's cross'd Temptation leads a person to pray for incompatible desires: one heaven-directed, the other wicked.
lying by the violet in the sun The radiance of the sun causes the violet to flourish and carrion (dead flesh) to grow putrid. Angelo thinks of Isabella as the violet, brought to flower by a sacred radiance, whereas he seems himself as corrupted by her virtuous purity.
lightness Sexual frivolity.
Having waste ground enough Why do I seek to build a privy on sacred ground (Isabella), when there is sufficient waste ground upon which this might be done? Angelo tries to come to terms with his desire to corrupt a pure woman, when there are sufficient impure women upon whom he might sate his lust.
art and nature Angelo never found himself tempted by the inherent sexuality and artful tricks of the whore.
fond Infatuated.

Act II Scene 3

The Duke, in his disguise as a friar, arrives at the prison. He meets Juliet and the Provost. Playing his part to the full, Vincentio ascertains the genuineness of Juliet's repentance and then leaves to visit Claudio with some 'instruction'. Juliet is distraught at the prospect of her lover's execution.

Commentary

The arrival of the Duke, disguised as the friar, brings a new and welcome note into the play. The chaos and uncertainty which Angelo has initiated in seeking to purge Vienna, gives way to an atmosphere of calm and reassurance. Partly, we may attribute this to the presence of the Duke, which gives us some hope that wrongs can be righted, and all made good in the end. But it is what the Dukes says *and* the way he says it that provides most reassurance. He speaks to Juliet in a sympathetic manner – he treats her as an individual. Quietly, he ascertains the genuineness of her repentance, whilst at the same time acknowledging that she has sinned. He is not concerned to offer at this stage any easy hope for the future, but he does offer her the comfort of confession, rather than brutal condemnation as a 'fornicatress'. He bids her 'rest'. He will seek to bring comfort to Claudio, and departs with a blessing on his lips. Sanity has entered the world. Christian charity has been granted to a hapless sinner.

flaws Flaming passions.
blister'd her report Damaged her own good name. Whores were branded on their foreheads.
you carry Refers to Juliet's pregnancy.
arraign Interrogate.
ourselves i.e. merely self-pity.
Showing . . . in fear Implies that true repentance must be for the sorrow we cause to God, rather than for the suffering we cause ourselves.
instruction i.e. spiritual advice.
respites Grants me the respite of my life.

Act II Scene 4

The scene begins with Angelo seeking to resolve his inner turmoil. One part of him seeks to pray, but he is racked by the torment of his passion for Isabella.

Isabella returns to continue her pleading for her brother's life. When she learns that there is to be no reprieve, she begs that time may be granted for Claudio to prepare his soul for death. Angelo, still unyielding, poses her a hypothetical question: would Isabella be prepared to give her body so that Claudio might be saved? Isabella replies that she would rather give her body than lose her soul. Angelo presses her still further: would such an act be accounted a sin? Isabella, little realizing where the argument is leading, replies that to surrender the body in such circumstances could not be accounted sin, rather it would be a manifestation of the Christian virtue of charity. Angelo now becomes direct and, taking Isabella at her word, suggests that Claudio could be reprieved if *she* would surrender her body to him – by her own previous admission it would be charitable so to do. Faced with reality rather than hypothesis, Isabella retracts: it would be better that Claudio should die than she should imperil her immortal soul by so foul an act. By now it is beginning to dawn upon her that she is in a trap. In the course of the conversation with Angelo, Isabella has been forced to minimize her brother's sin, in order to excuse him – now it is becoming apparent that she is being asked to commit a similar offence. She excuses her change of heart by drawing attention to the frailty of womankind. At this point, it is apparent to Angelo that Isabella has not quite realized what is being asked of her. He announces that he loves her and that her surrender to him is the price that must be paid for Claudio's life. Horrified, Isabella threatens to denounce Angelo; he merely points out that, such is his reputation, no one would believe her. She has until tomorrow to make up her mind. Angelo threatens that he will torture Claudio. Distraught because of the horror of her predicament, Isabella decides that she cannot surrender her chastity and thus her brother must die – she will go to him and prepare him for his death. She feels confident that Claudio will understand her decision – he would rather die twenty times over than that *she* should permit herself to be defiled so that *he* might be saved.

Commentary

In his soliloquy, Angelo reveals himself to be a man driven by a fearful compulsion. He would control his desires, but he cannot: 'Blood, thou art blood.' False-seeming must now govern his behaviour. Characteristically, he employs the lawyer's wiles to trap Isabella into yielding to his desires. He presents a hypothetical case as an example of a way that Claudio might be saved (involving the yielding of a hypothetical virginity by a hypothetical girl) and attempts to trick Isabella into agreeing that such a course might be permissible. He appeals to the apparent lightness with which Isabella treats unchastity (in pleading for her brother's life) in order to suggest that chastity itself is a light matter. Isabella is asked to behave in a manner true to her sex and demonstrate 'frailty'. All his equivocation is met either with incomprehension, or forceful counter-argument, by the inviolable Isabella. Eventually, he is forced to break cover and declare his love for her. Isabella's first reaction is that this is another trick to lead her on, but she comes at last to face the horror of the reality: she may save her brother, if she yields her virginity and becomes Angelo's lover. Shakespeare has here shown us the workings of tyranny. Fundamentally, Angelo seeks to bend Isabella to his will. The tyranny becomes most blatant when he threatens Claudio not only with death, but also with torture before he is executed. The reality that Angelo will be able to shrug off Isabella's public denunciation of him, on the strength of his reputation, rings horribly true, and highlights the vulnerability of her situation.

In the face of all this pressure, Isabella is outraged but unyielding. To modern ears, her resolute clinging to her chastity may seem unreasonable – after all, her brother's life is at stake. We must take seriously, however, her contention that to give way to Angelo would imperil her immortal soul. Also we must remember that she is a novice, who therefore would be expected to put a sacred value on her virginity. There remains a nagging question, though. Might not the surrender of her body represent a form of Christian sacrifice – after all, such a sin, if it be a sin, would hardly carry much weight, especially as it would have been forced upon her? And surely it is arguable that chastity is a spiritual condition rather than linked inevitably to the physical condition of remaining a virgin? If we follow this line, then Isabella's action, in defending her physical virginity, becomes as absolutist as Angelo's view of the world. Some critics have been led to the conclusion that Isabella's outrage springs from an aversion to physical sex and fear for her reputation, rather than from a true understanding of spiritual values.

To several subjects On many different subjects.
invention Thought.
conception i.e. about Isabella.
sere Withered.
boot Advantage.
idle Useless.
case Outward appearance.
habit Appearance.
Blood Passion.
good angel . . . crest Angelo suggests that although he may appear to have an appearance of goodness, it is not the reality.
teach Show.
muster Gather.
untaught Ignorant.
offence Offensive.
fitted Adjusted.
from nature stolen i.e. taken life, committed murder.
already made i.e. created.
remit Pardon.
saucy sweetness Lecherous pleasure.
coin Beget.
mettle Spirit.
restrained means Forbidden instruments.
compell'd sins Sins we are forced to commit.
accompt Truly reckoned.
charity Love.
tax Reprove.

black masks Refers to the nun's veil.
enciel'd Enshielded.
gross Blatantly.
pain Penalty.
die for ever i.e. suffer an eternity in hell.
Ignomy Ignominy, shame.
two houses Of different origins.
sliding Moral laxity.
merriment Trifle.
something Somewhat.
feodary Confederate.
owe Own.
glasses Mirrors.
forms Images.
profiting Taking advantage of.
credulous to false prints i.e. women are easily susceptible to false impressions.
the destin'd livery i.e. that which women inevitably are composed of.
licence Liberty.
To pluck on others To test out the resolution of others.
Outstretched i.e. wide-open.
Unsoil'd Unsullied (reputation).
vouch Guarantee of my probity.
calumny Falsity.
sensual race the rein Give full rein to my lusts.
nicety Modesty.
prolixious Excessive.
banish what they sue for i.e. Angelo finds her modesty provocative.
sufferance Suffering.
approof Approval.
make curtsey Be subservient to.
prompture Prompting.
blood Sexual passion.

Revision questions on Act II

1 Compare and contrast the attitudes of Escalus and Angelo in Scene 1.

2 What arguments does Isabella use in her plea to save Claudio, and how does Angelo counter them?

3 'More than our brother is our chastity.' How far do you find yourself able to sympathize with Isabella's point of view?

4 Describe the relationship of the comic sub-plot to the main plot as it appears in the first scene of the act.

5 Do you think that Shakespeare presents Angelo as a psychologically convincing character in Act II?

Act III Scene 1

Claudio humbly thanks 'Friar' Vincentio for the comfort he has given him as he faces death; it consisted of a number of ruminations on the inevitability of death and the transitoriness of worldly joys. As the Duke departs, promising to visit Claudio again, Isabella arrives. She brings bad news: there is no mercy in Angelo; but she also reveals that if she would relinquish her virginity, then Claudio might be spared. Isabella is confident that Claudio will find this remedy as repellent as she does – and for a moment it looks as though she has judged the matter rightly. After a short hesitation, however, he changes his mind: if the moralistic Angelo regards the sin of fornication so lightly, then if he is right, Claudio can see no reason for his sister not to surrender her honour – and death, surely, is a 'fearful thing'. Isabella is outraged to find that her brother is prepared to contemplate her shame as the price for his life, and she roundly condemns him: 'O faithless coward! O dishonest wretch!' In her eyes, he is no better than Angelo; it would be best for him to die quickly.

The Duke reappears, having overheard this conversation, and asks to be left alone with Isabella. It now becomes apparent that the Duke sees the truth about the man whom he left as his deputy: he is not the first man to have fallen from grace through frailty. Isabella tells Vincentio that she is going to Angelo to reject his offer and to threaten to denounce him publicly. The Duke asks her to follow a different course: he has a plan which will preserve Isabella's honour, save Claudio and set right the wrong done to an innocent woman. Isabella agrees to listen. It appears that Angelo was once promised in marriage to Mariana, but before the contract could have the blessing of the Church, her brother was lost at sea – thus depriving the hapless girl of her dowry. As a consequence, Angelo refused to solemnize the marriage and rejected the girl. Since this catastrophe she has lived in retirement, but her love for Angelo has remained unabated. In fact, paradoxically, the more she feels spurned the more she loves him. The Duke proposes that Isabella should go to Angelo and agree to meet him by night in a secluded place. When Angelo arrives, expecting to have his way with Isabella, in fact, he will meet Mariana. He will not appreciate the substitution that has taken place because of the darkness. Isabella is prepared to put her trust in the idea.

Commentary

The Duke's opening speech is somewhat out of character in the sense that it represents thematically what might be termed the familiar arguments on the transitoriness and travail of earthly life. The ideas may be clichéd, but they are stated with a concreteness of imagery (typical of the Duke) which gives them great power. In a sense, the Duke speaks here as a chorus or commentator who presents a view of death that contrasts vividly with the sensuous description of the horrors of death, which is uttered by Claudio a little later in the scene. By the time that Vincentio has finished his address, Claudio pronounces himself adjusted to the idea of his own death. His calm is short-lived.

Isabella now enters and immediately Claudio asks 'What comfort?' Despite all that he has heard from the 'Friar', he still expects 'remedy'. It is worth emphasizing that the Duke overhears all the ensuing conversation. Isabella's notion that Claudio might consider himself as a 'swift ambassador' to heaven (presumably bearing witness to the devilishness of Angelo) seems oddly-conceived and lacking in human sympathy for his predicament. As Isabella proceeds to unfold her story, it becomes apparent that she is unwilling to reveal immediately the proposal which Angelo has made to her. When revelation does come, she has prepared the ground – and gets the answer which she wishes to receive. But the consolation is short-lived, once the reality of his situation has dawned on Claudio. Claudio's speech about the unknown horrors which may lie beyond the grave (reminiscent of Hamlet) show him to be acutely in love with life, and contrast vividly with the sententious utterances of the Duke, which opened the scene. The fact that neither the Duke nor Isabella have managed to reconcile this young man to his fate intensifies the drama. Although momentarily Claudio is prepared to support his sister's decision not to yield her body, as soon as he reflects on the situation we find that he restates the view expressed earlier by Angelo: a compelled sin may not be regarded as sin at all, and, if it is sinful to yield the body, then surely it is the least deadly of the seven sins. Angelo, ironically, in being prepared to commit this sin, unwittingly, becomes a witness for his defence.

An impasse has been reached and Isabella falls back on outright denunciation of her brother's cowardice. At this point, many critics have found Isabella entirely repulsive in her heartlessness towards her brother. Surely there is a more humane way to handle the matter, other than by ranting and self-concern (for her 'shame', be it noted)? Psychologically her attitude may be defended by suggesting that her anger and contempt is really anger with herself, which has to find an outlet – and Claudio (a man, and using some of the arguments of Angelo) is the nearest person to hand. But in clinging to her chastity she shows a far from admirable lack of the greater Christian virtue of charity.

We may thus see Claudio at this point as a victim of two essentially sterile absolutes: legalism and chastity. Ironically, Angelo and Isabella are linked – both present a warm, living being with the prospect of becoming 'a kneaded clod'. In both cases their standpoint is theoretical; Claudio alone represents suffering humanity – it is only with him that we can wholly identify.

The time has come for the Duke to intervene. His function is essentially educative. He does not intervene directly to set matters right but suggests that Isabella must *do* something. The necessity of her going to Angelo and seeming to agree to his proposal involves a compromise of her standards. But this she is prepared to do – putting her faith in the overall reassurance of the 'Friar' that she will not suffer dishonour. We need not be disquieted unduly by the deception involved: in performing his function as a wise ruler, it may be regarded as permissible for the Duke to employ cunning to promote virtue and discountenance evil. According to contemporary theories of government, in such instances, the end may be regarded as justifying the means.

absolute Resolved.
skyey Astrological.
habitation . . . keep'st i.e. the earth.
Death's fool Made a fool of by death.
yet run'st . . . still Death mocks any attempt at evasion. No matter how fast you run from death, you cannot put yourself any the further from it.
accommodations Trappings of the world.
nurs'd by baseness Composed of earthly matter, sustained by it, and by implication must return to it.
fork Tongue.
work Snake.
grossly Mightily.

certain i.e. there is no certainty.
complexion Temperament.
After the moon According to the phases of the moon.
bowels Offspring.
proper True.
serpigo Herpes, or ringworm.
rheum Watery discharge.
after-dinner's sleep Life is similar to an after-dinner nap, when the events of the morning are mingled with dreams of what we may do in the evening.
blessed youth . . . eld The sense here is dependent upon the pun 'arms' and 'alms'. The paralyzed old seek arms from the young, whereas impoverished youth begs alms from the old.
heat Sexual desire.
affection Passion.
limb Refers to any bodily organ.
pleasant Enjoyable.
yet Still.
odds all even i.e. death evens out all the inequalities of life.
leiger Emissary.
durance Imprisonment.
vastidity Immensity.
To a determin'd scope Confined limit.
bark Strip the bark from.
trunk (a) body and (b) the trunk of a tree.
entertain Maintain.
corporal sufferance Bodily, physical suffering.
flowery i.e. flowery language.
appliances Compromises.
settl'd visage Fixed expression.
Nips . . . fowl A hawking metaphor. The hawk kills its victim by 'nipping' its head. 'enew'=put down.
cast Possibly, 'cast forth'.
precise Puritanical.
guards Outward shows.
rank Heinous.
still i.e. Angelo would grant Claudio permission to carry on offending, so long as Isabella continued to yield her honour.
frankly Generously, freely.
bite . . . nose Treat the law with contempt.
trick Trifle.
perdurably fin'd Punished eternally.
cold obstruction Refers to the cold inactivity of the dead body.
sensible Capable of feeling sensations.
motion Refers to the activity of the living body.
kneaded clod i.e. the body is made one with the earth.
thrilling Stinging, piercing.
viewless Invisible.

pendent The world was sometimes pictured as hanging from Heaven by a golden chain.
those . . . howling Refers to the underworld as portrayed in classical literature. Pre-Christian – therefore 'lawless'. 'Incertain'= undisciplined imagination.
penury Poverty.
Heaven shield . . . blood Isabella casts aspersions on the parenthood of Claudio: 'Surely he can't be the legitimate son of her father!'
shield Forbid.
warped slip of wilderness Offspring of wild stock.
it i.e. execution.
a trade i.e. an accustomed way of life.
Mercy . . . bawd Mercy (personified) if it were granted to you would, in effect, be an accomplice to your lecherousness.
Vouchsafe Grant.
disposition Control.
cheap i.e. is easily come by.
soul . . . complexion Essence of your nature.
body Outward appearance.
assault i.e. upon your virtue.
resolve him Tell him straight.
affianced Pledged to marry her.
solemnity i.e. the solemnization of the marriage.
wracked Wrecked.
heavily Sadly.
sinew i.e. the essential part of.
combinate Contracted (by the marriage-arrangement).
swallowed Retracted.
bestowed . . . lamentation Deserted her, to suffer her own grief.
avail Benefit.
rupture Breach.
to the point In every detail.
refer . . . advantage Consider yourself only advantaged in that . . .
stead up Keep the appointment in your stead.
acknowledge itself hereafter Comes to be publicly acknowledged.
scaled Weighed in the scales of justice.
frame Prepare.
attempt Assault.
carry this i.e. carry this off.
image Idea.
holding up Ability to see it through.
grange Country house.

Act III Scene 2

Pompey, under arrest and in the charge of Elbow and some officers, meets the 'Friar'. On hearing that Pompey is a bawd, the

Duke condemns his 'filthy vice' and tells Froth to see that he is taken to prison. Lucio, who now arrives on the scene, is equally happy to see Pompey imprisoned – despite the evident pleasure that he himself takes in whoring. The luckless Pompey is led away – his impertinent pleas for leniency have proved fruitless: no one is willing to stand bail for him.

Lucio enquires of the 'Friar' if he has heard any news of the Duke. Vincentio replies that he knows nothing of his whereabouts! The conversation proceeds to a consideration of the merits of the 'absent' Duke. Lucio laments his absence: it has brought about the regime of Angelo, who, Lucio is convinced, owes his conception to the mating of two stock-fish. Various other doubts are cast on the parentage and sexuality of Angelo; Lucio is of the belief that the Duke, on the other hand, as well as being complaisant about lechery, is himself a confirmed womanizer. Not surprisingly, the 'Friar' is moved to disagree with this opinion – Lucio is either deceived or malicious. As the slanders mount, so the Duke becomes more vigorous in his self-defence. Lucio swears that he is prepared to hold to his accusations, even if the Duke were to return. The 'Friar' replies that he had better hope that Vincentio does *not* return. Lucio next asks if it is true that Claudio is to die tomorrow; affecting to know nothing of the matter, the 'Friar' asks why this should come to pass. Lucio states Claudio's crime, whilst lamenting the absence of the Duke, who would surely be lenient over such matters. Lucio departs.

Mistress Overdone next appears; she too is under arrest. With her comes Escalus, who has gleaned sufficient evidence to effect her imprisonment: Lucio has been his informant. Mistress Overdone denounces Lucio, whilst informing Escalus that she has taken responsibility for Lucio's child – begotten of Mistress Kate Keep-down, a woman who was subsequently deserted by her lover despite the fact that he had contracted to marry her. A parallel is thus established between Angelo, Claudio and Lucio: all have undertaken marriage contracts which have been broken. In the case of Angelo and Lucio this forswearing was an act of heartlessness.

After the departure of Mistress Overdone, Escalus orders the Provost to arraign Lucio. Left alone with Escalus, the 'Friar' bemoans the way the world is going, and then 'innocently' enquires the opinion of Escalus concerning the Duke. He receives the reply that he was a man who contrived 'especially to know himself' and was a 'gentleman of all temperance'. It may be imagined that this opinion reassures him greatly, after the slanders uttered by Lucio. The kindly Escalus asks after Claudio. The 'Friar' replies that he has brought him comfort and that he is now composed to meet his death. Escalus clearly finds Angelo too harsh in his judgements.

In rhymed couplets, alone on the stage, the Duke comments that those who administer severe justice must needs be equally severe with themselves. Angelo stands condemned because he condemns others for faults of which he himself is guilty – in short, he is a hypocrite. The Duke looks forward to the working-out of the 'Mariana scheme'.

Commentary

After the intensity of the previous scene, with its potential for tragedy, the reassurance provided by the comedy of this scene is surely welcome. Pompey represents the vice-ridden society which the Duke left behind him when he went into 'retirement'. In his disguise as the Friar, he is roundly condemnatory of the licentious world in general, and Pompey in particular. His remarks, which are given prominence by being in verse, would to some extent be applicable to Angelo. His desire that Pompey should be taken off to prison indicates that it is one of the functions of authority to see that the wicked are punished. His merciful attitude towards Claudio shows the need for authority to discriminate between the great sin and the venial slip. Angelo has condemned all alike.

But, of course, the mood is essentially comic. His problem with Lucio, who persists in slandering him, is simply funny. Lucio's reference to the coldness of Angelo underlines the essential frigidity of the deputy's nature. Whatever we may think of the world of Pompey and Lucio – it at least has the merit of colour and life. To attempt to dam up the natural impulses of man is shown to be an unrealistic folly. Not that we should be carried away by Lucio's good humour and jokes: we learn that he, like Claudio and Angelo, has contracted a clandestine marriage. Also, he shares the dubious distinction with Angelo of having broken his contract, and let the girl down. Lucio's insolence also presents the Duke in rather a different light from the one we have seen him in hitherto. He may be a controlling, even Providential figure, in the previous scene. In this scene we have seen him dispensing judgement. But Lucio's picture of him as 'mad, fantastical' brings him down to earth. Also, his Providential status is further diminished as we watch him having to suffer the indignities of Lucio's slanders. His disguise prevents him from being able to deny what Lucio says (for the moment). He is thus forced to suffer in silence and with mounting annoyance.

After Lucio's departure, the Duke is given some respite during his conversation with Escalus: his ruffled feathers are soothed and dignity restored. The rhymed couplets at the end of the scene form a generalized choric comment on the play so far, and indicate what will happen in the near future.

world . . . bastard As well as the more familiar meaning, 'bastard' was also the name given to a sweet Spanish wine. The implication would seem to be that the whole world would be over-run by 'bastards'.
two usuries i.e. money-lending, and prostitution.
the merriest i.e. prostitution.
furred gown A rich garment – presumably one of the fruits of money-lending.
fox on lambskins Suggests that the low cunning of the usurer is concealed by the lamb-like innocence of outward demeanour.
pick-lock A bawdy reference – presumably it was used to pick the locks of chastity belts.
maw Belly.
prove his Pompey provides the devil with arguments for sin.
were as good It would be better for him (to take the longest way to see him) – thus delaying, at least, the inevitable punishment.
a cord, sir i.e. a cord will be used to hang Pompey, similar to the cord which goes around the friar's waist.
at the wheels of Caesar i.e. in a state of subjection. Historically, Pompey was not led through Rome in triumph.
Pygmalion Legend has it that Pygmalion made his statues come to life by falling in love with them.
newly made woman In early womanhood, a state of virginity.
extracting clutched A hand clutched in order to hold money.
drowned . . . rain Passed out of fashion.
trot Old crone.
The trick of it The way things go.
in the tub Where she might 'sweat out' her venereal infection. Also, beef was salted in a tub.
Ever your fresh whore The implication is that young workers become 'madams' later in life.
powdered 'Powdered' beef was another name for salted beef. Whores of course would make liberal use of powder as make-up.
unshunned Unavoidable.
house i.e. the prison, where Pompey will now be 'kept'.
the wear The fashion.

mettle Courage.
usurp the beggary Some commentators think that this remark indicates that Lucio sees through the Duke's disguise. More likely, it is an unconscious irony.
puts . . . to't i.e. he puts it down.
crabbed Harsh.
extirp it quite Wipe it out completely.
downright Normal, down-to-earth.
stockfishes Cod.
motion unregenerative A puppet, unable to reproduce itself. The implication is that Angelo is sterile and impotent.
pleasant Jesting.
rebellion of a codpiece Fornication, sexual indulgence.
nursing a thousand One supposes that the Duke is not impressed by this back-handed compliment.
the sport Sexual sport.
clack-dish Beggars 'clacked' the lid of their begging bowls. A bawdy euphemism for the female sex organs.
inward In his confidence.
the greater file Most of his subjects.
unweighing Not given to good judgement.
envy Malice.
helmed Conducted.
upon . . . need Should the need arise.
bringings-forth Deeds.
darkened Obscured.
honest True.
forswear Gainsay.
tun-dish A funnel, hence the male sex-organ.
ungenitured Sterile.
darkly Secretly.
untrussing 'Taking his trousers down'. Removing his hose.
eat mutton on Fridays i.e. do something which is forbidden. 'Mutton' is a slang term for a whore.
mouth Kiss.
mortality Human life.
censure Judgement.
Back-wounding Backbiting.
gall Maliciousness.
Philip and Jacob Refers to their 'Saints Day' – May 1st.
divines Clergymen.
entertainment Reception.
See The Holy See – Rome.
fever . . . cure it Goodness is so stricken (with a 'fever') that can only be cured by death.
Novelty Used in the sense of 'a craving for newness'.
secure Free from care.
security i.e. the sort of security for moneys owed.

fellowships accurst Enterprises are threatened by exorbitant demands for security.
temperance Moderation.
events Business.
sinister Unjust.
framed to himself Formed in his own mind.
instruction . . . frailty As a response to the instructions of his weaknesses.
deceiving . . . life Many deceptive notions about what life has to offer.
discredited to him Disabused him of.
shore Limit.
answer i.e. so long as his own strictness with himself is matched by his strictness with others.
to stand To be of moral standing.
go Upon which he may base his own proceedings.
Than . . . weighing Meting out punishment to others no more severely than is appropriate to his own faults.
my vice i.e. the vice present in other people.
How . . . the times This is an obscure passage; the text is corrupt at this point. Many editors presume that a couplet is missing.
practice Deceit.
Pay with falsehood false exacting The false Isabella (Mariana) shall pay with treachery the treacherous dealings of Angelo.

Revision questions on Act III

1 Indicate Claudio's changes in response as Isabella unfolds the full story of her interview with Angelo.

2 How far do you find yourself in sympathy with Isabella in the first scene of the act?

3 Why do you think that the Duke does not unmask himself to Claudio and Isabella, thereby saving a great deal of heartache and risking potential disaster?

4 Discuss the part played by Lucio in Scene 2.

5 Show how our perception of the Duke changes during the course of this act.

Act IV Scene 1

Mariana is listening to a love-song. The Duke, in his disguise as Friar, arrives – he is expecting Isabella. When she comes, the Duke asks Mariana to leave them for a moment. He learns from Isabella that she has performed the task which he gave her: she has appeared to consent to Angelo, and she has received directions from him concerning the place of assignation: a conveniently secluded and walled garden. She is to meet him by night. The Duke is satisfied with the arrangements, Mariana is recalled, and she retires with Isabella to be informed of the arrangements which have been made. The Duke has time for a few remarks on the wickedness of slander. Isabella returns with Mariana, who is happy to consent to the Duke's plan.

Commentary

This scene is chiefly concerned with forwarding the plot. The song at the beginning, although it tells of false love, nonetheless prefigures a new harmony which is about to be brought about by the Duke's machinations. Isabella's description of the precautions which Angelo took in showing her the way to the secret garden betoken his guilty conscience. Overall we see the operation of what the Duke has called 'craft against vice'. His soliloquy at the end of the scene would appear to have little direct relevance, but may show him to be still smarting over the innuendoes which he suffered at the hands of Lucio.

Song Some commentators do not attribute this song to Shakespeare.
brawling Clamorous.
circummur'd Walled round.
planched Planked.
his Its.
on From.
wary Careful.
action . . . precept Angelo gave her precise directions – verbally and not by means of demonstration? An obscure phrase.
possess'd Informed.
borne up Contrived.
place . . . greatness i.e. those who are highly-placed and great.
false eyes i.e. subject to the gaze of those who are treacherous.
contrarious quests Conflicting debates.
Upon About.
escapes of wit i.e. the mighty are made the subject of countless fantasies.
rack Torture.
pre-contract Refers to their betrothal.
Sith Since.
flourish Embellish.
tithe's i.e. that portion of the corn which represents the taxation which must be paid.

Act IV Scene 2

Pompey, in the prison at last, is offered the job of executioner's assistant by the Provost: Abhorson, the local hangman, 'lacks a helper'. Pompey accepts the post and has a brief discussion with Abhorson about the nature of the hangman's craft. Claudio is to be executed with one Barnardine, a convicted murderer. After some initial outrage that he is being asked to share his mystery with a simple bawd, Abhorson leaves with Pompey, to instruct him in the hangman's trade.

The Provost asks that Claudio and Barnardine be summoned. Claudio arrives to say that Barnardine cannot be roused from a deep slumber. There is a knocking. Claudio is dispatched to prepare himself for execution. The 'Friar' enters; he is surprised to hear that Isabella has not yet arrived at the prison, but his subsequent words express some hope that Claudio may be saved. More knocking arouses expectation in the Friar and the Provost that a reprieve is at hand – surely the messenger, who is admitted, brings a pardon from Angelo? But no, he brings a letter to the Provost, which orders the execution of Claudio at 4 a.m., to be followed by the death of Barnardine in the following afternoon. The Duke's hopes seem to be about to be frustrated. A way out, however, presents itself: the Duke suggests that the wicked Barnadine be executed first, and that after some suitable adjustments, the head should be sent to Angelo. If the plan works the Duke may be able to buy some time – success depends upon Angelo being made to believe that Barnardine's head is Claudio's. The switch will naturally involve great risks for the Provost. The Duke pacifies his fears by assuring him that Vincentio intends to return in two days' time and a letter is produced, bearing the Duke's seal, and in the Duke's handwriting, which confirms the imminent return of Vincentio.

As morning approaches, the Duke goes off to bring spiritual comfort to the hardened criminal, Barnardine.

Commentary

In this scene we witness the coming together of Pompey, the bawd, and Abhorson, the hangman. The very name 'Abhorson' – a linkage of 'abhor' and 'whoreson' – suggests how Shakespeare intends we should regard him, and links him, incidentally, with the trade of Pompey. Both Pompey and Abhorson represent the bottom rungs of respective ladders: Pompey exploits human weakness and Abhorson is the final executant of Justice.

A right-thinking society, whilst perhaps acknowledging their necessity, regards both professions with distaste, and prefers to avert its gaze. Although, in a sense, they are on opposite sides of the fence (Justice/Criminality), there is much truth in the Provost's comment: 'Go to, sir, you weigh equally: a feather will turn the scale.' This is a worldly-wise assessment on all levels of unregenerate human society.

There is also reference to the sleeping Barnardine. He, like Claudio, is under sentence of death. But there the similarity ends: Barnardine is a hardened murderer, who, it is implied, deserves to die, whereas Claudio is relatively innocent. Also, it may be noted that Barnardine, at this moment, seems blissfully untroubled by the sentence which hangs over him, whereas Claudio expressed utter horror at the prospect of his own extinction. Thus they represent opposite ends of the spectrum of human feelings about death.

The news that Angelo requires Claudio to be executed much earlier than expected represents a serious hitch in the Duke's plans. He may have Providential attributes, but he is certainly not omniscient. At once, however, a solution presents itself: Barnardine shall die in place of Claudio – and Barnadine's head shall be suitably disguised and sent to Angelo. Much is made of Barnardine's unregenerate state of mind (and the impossibility of bringing him to repentance), in order to relieve any moral odium which might be attached to the revised plan. We are not invited to lose any sleep over Barnardine's death.

Finally, the scene ends on a note of hope: the Duke's 'return' is imminent – it is 'almost clear dawn'.

snatches Witticisms, quibbles.
gyves Fetters.
compound Come to an agreement with.
estimation Reputation.
mystery Craft.
favour A pun on the obvious meaning of the word, and 'favour' – meaning 'face'.
a hanging look Another pun. (a) doleful expression, (b) an obvious reference to his calling.
Painting . . . mystery Painting is a trade (mystery), whores apply paint to their faces, they are obviously companions of Pompey – thus he can claim to be a practitioner of a 'mystery'.
Every true man's apparel . . . thief Abhorson's argument is obscure – part of it seems to be missing!
forgiveness The hangman used to ask for the forgiveness of his victims.

a good turn A pun which depends upon the fact that hangmen were said to 'turn off' their victims when they removed the ladder from them at the gallows.
starkly Stiffly.
curfew i.e. the prison bell, to denote the onset of night.
stroke and line Angelo's life is mirrored exactly in his justice.
qualify Modify, lessen.
meal'd Mixed up with (that which he corrects in others).
Unsisting Probably 'unshifting', but there is some debate about this word amongst editors.
postern A small, but strong door.
countermand Reprieve.
siege Seat.
Profess'd . . . contrary Expressed himself opposed to it.
offence . . . authority Offences are soon pardoned when they owe their origins to those who possess high authority.
When . . . friended When those who are vice-ridden are merciful, the vicious are befriended because their vice is loved.
putting-on Urging.
nine years old i.e. he has been a prisoner for nine years.
fact Crime.
undoubtful proof Until now there was some doubt about his guilt.
touched Affected.
mortality Death.
desperately mortal With no hope of immortality.
advice i.e. spiritual advice.
cunning Skill.
I will lay myself in hazard I will take the risk.
in . . . effect In a clearly demonstrable manner.
I may . . . Claudio's I risk a similar fate to that of Claudio.
discover the favour Realize the difference in their faces.
tie Possibly means 'trim'.
avouch Acknowledge.
character Handwriting.
what is writ Refers to the letter denoting the return of the Duke, which the Provost has been asked to read at his leisure.
th' unfolding star i.e. the morning star, which signals to shepherds that it is time to fetch their sheep from the sheep-fold.
resolve Reassure.

Act IV Scene 3

Pompey recalls some of the people whom he has met in the prison; Angelo's clean-up of the city has obviously been proceeding apace. He is interrupted by Abhorson, who orders him to summon Barnardine forth for execution. Barnardine, however, heavy with sleep refuses to budge. Eventually, he emerges from his straw – but he still obstinately refuses to prepare himself for his death. The 'Friar' arrives and tries his hand at persuasion, but Barnardine is not to be persuaded and makes off. The Provost enters and demands that Barnardine be brought to the block. By this time, however, the 'Friar' is forced to admit that to execute such an impenitent character would be damnable. The Duke's plan is going awry: the Claudio-substitute refuses to comply with his wishes. Matters are saved by the Provost, who suggests that the pirate Ragozine – recently dead of a fever – should supply the missing head. Fortunately, he bears an even greater resemblance to Claudio than the recalcitrant Barnardine – thus there is the greater likelihood of Angelo being deceived. The 'Friar' is pleased and orders the dispatch of the head. He tells the Provost to conceal Claudio and Barnardine until further notice. The Provost is reassured: he was naturally fearful that Angelo might discover that his orders had not been carried out. Alone for a moment, the Duke determines to write letters to Angelo denoting his imminent return and telling Angelo that he must meet him at 'the consecrated fount, a league below the city'. The Provost returns with the head of Ragozine; the Duke inspects it briefly; the Provost departs to deliver it to Angelo.

On hearing the approach of Isabella, the Duke decides to conceal from her his plans and promptly informs her, to her distress and outrage, that Claudio has already been executed. To comfort her the 'Friar' tells her that he has heard of the Duke's return; if she can be patient, she is promised she may revenge herself upon Angelo. She consents to be directed by the 'Friar'. Isabella then departs with a letter for Friar Peter, asking for his presence that night at the house of Mariana. Lucio arrives, just as Isabella is leaving and is distressed by her evident signs of woe. When she has gone, Lucio continues his slanders against the Duke and unwittingly corroborates Mistress Overdone's story about his 'getting a wench with child'. The Duke is still not amused to hear Lucio's version of his character. They depart together, with Lucio promising to stick to him 'like a burr'.

Commentary

Barnardine refuses to co-operate: 'I will not die today for any man's persuasion.' The Duke's well-laid scheme encounters another hitch. Fortunately Ragozine's head is available to be sent to Angelo. At this point in the play the note of black comedy is most apparent. The Duke covers up his failure to persuade Barnardine to die by saying that he was not fitted for death anyway – a touch of sour grapes? In 'saving' Barnardine Shakespeare diverged from his source, and it is reasonable to suppose that there was a reason. It is thought that Shakespeare was unwilling to kill off such a lovable rogue, but there may be something more to it than this. Shakespeare, in frustrating the Duke's wishes, seems to be saying that not even a beneficent ruler has the right to use a man's life for his own convenience. It is hinted that this is a lesson that the Duke has to learn. In the comedy the point is made, nonetheless. Ironically, in seeking to sacrifice Barnardine on the altar of convenience, the Duke is not all that far away from the standpoint adopted by Angelo with reference to Claudio.

We may find it hard to stomach the Duke's lie to Isabella saying that Claudio has been executed, although by this time we have learned to 'trust' his deviousness is all in a good cause. Nonetheless, it does cause her gratuitous suffering. Once again, the demands of the story are paramount and we are asked to avert our eyes from such troublous questions. Thematically, one supposes, it may be part of Isabella's education that she should come to plead even for Angelo's life, without the knowledge that her brother lives – an exercise of Christian charity, indeed.

Once more Lucio is presented engagingly: at the end of the scene, he sympathetically seeks to comfort Isabella, and his stinging remarks about the 'absent' Duke amuse us greatly.

our house of profession i.e. whorehouse.
commodity . . . pounds Refers to a dishonest practice of money-lenders. A sum would be lent, and the debtor would have to accept part of the principle in the form of worthless 'commodities' – such as ginger and brown paper. Thus the usurer could evade the statutory 10% interest rate.
Caper Young men liked to 'cut a caper' at dancing, by means of agile leaps.
peaches Accuses.
Deep-vow Swearer of prodigious oaths.
Copperspur Refers to the practice of making copper look like gold.
rapier and dagger man Fashionable weapons – for show rather than action.
Drop-heir Pimp.
Shoe-tie It was fashionable to decorate shoes with rosettes – a foreign affectation, hence the reference to travelling.
Half-can Refers possibly to the dishonest practice of making false quantity-markings on ale-pots.

'for . . . sake' Traditionally the cry of begging prisoners, uttered through the bars of their jail.
rise A pun: 'rise from your bed', and also 'mount the scaffold'.
clap Hasten (to your prayers).
betimes Early.
ghostly Spiritual.
billets Logs used for burning.
ward Cell.
gravel i.e. stony.
unmeet Unfitted.
transport i.e. to the after-life.
omit Ignore.
Prefix'd Ordained.
continue Allow (Claudio) to continue his life.
holds Cells.
journal Daily.
To yonder generation i.e. those who are outside the prison.
free Innocent.
cold gradation Impersonal logic.
well-balanc'd form With proper attention to the formalities.
Convenient Suitable.
ignorant of her good i.e. her good fortune. The Duke's reason for keeping her in ignorance answers more the demands of the plot than Isabella's spirituality.
patience Ability to accept suffering. A Christian virtue.
Forbear Cease.
instance News.
bosom i.e. your wishes (concerning Angelo).
head Face.
combined Bound.
fretting The idea is that the tears are wearing channels in her cheeks.
pervert Misdirect.
fain Forced.
bran Bran bread.
for my head To keep my head (from the executioner).
set me to't Provoke my sexual urge.
fantastical Given to wild imagination.
duke of dark corners Lucio maintains his slander: Vincentio was given to keeping secret trysts with lovers. In fact, the remark is ironical in view of the 'spying out' that the Duke has done during the course of the play.
marvellous little beholding Consciously ironical.
lives not i.e. is not to be found (recognized) in Lucio's reports of him.
woodman Hunter (of women).
forswear Deny.
medlar A sort of apple which is only edible when partly rotten – hence a term for a prostitute.
honest Honourable.

burr The prickly head of the burdock which sticks to the clothes.

Act IV Scene 4

Letters received from the Duke have confused Angelo and Escalus. They understand that they have to meet Vincentio at the city gates. Their orders are to alert any who have grievances to be present. Left alone, Angelo has a presentiment that all is not going too well for him: he feels guilty for his defloration (as he thinks) of Isabella but he is confident that she will not denounce him because of her sense of shame. He also feels that nobody would believe her, in any case. Angelo also expresses some guilt for the 'death' of Claudio – he invents another reason for having him executed: he would have denounced Angelo on account of his remorse for Isabella's sacrifice.

Commentary

There is an overriding sense of confusion in this scene. First there is the uncertainty over the import of the Duke's letters, which in any case have been contradictory. Significantly, Angelo shows particular anxiety about the Duke's desire that people should have the opportunity to seek redress for injustice. Angelo's soliloquy reveals a tortured mind: he feels remorseful for his supposed sin against Isabella, yet he reassures himself that his reputation will protect him against any accusations that may be levelled against him. He wishes Claudio had lived, yet he is glad that Claudio is dead so that he cannot denounce him. Thus we find Angelo at bay, the realization forced upon him that 'when once our grace we have forgot,/Nothing goes right; we would, and we would not.'

disvouched Contradicted.
uneven Unpredictable.
tainted Impaired.
dispatch Speedy settlement.
Betimes Early.
sort and suit i.e. men who have status enough to require a retinue.
unshapes Disorientates.
unpregnant Unready.
it Fornication, especially the deflowering of virgins.
tongue Speak against me.
credent bulk i.e. is of such massive credibility.
particular Personal.

confounds Destroys.
the breather The person who utters it.
sense Passion.
receiving . . . shame Refers to the fact that Claudio, had he lived, would have denounced Angelo because he would not have been able to bear the knowledge that he owed his life to his sister's shame.
grace Mercy.

Act IV Scene 5

The Duke has emerged from his disguise. Friar Peter is given letters to deliver and ordered to make further preparations for the Duke's return. He is to follow orders precisely. Varrius arrives and departs with Vincentio – they are going to meet various friends.

Commentary

In contrast to the previous scene, here there is a sense of purposeful activity. The Duke has dropped his disguise and now prepares for his formal arrival at the gates of Vienna. The audience's anticipation is aroused as we move towards the dénouement. These short scenes at the end of Act IV contribute a feeling of action – preparations are being made for the grand finale, although we do not know as yet how the Duke's plans are to arrive at their fruition.

me i.e. for me. Shakespeare forgot about these letters; later on Peter tells his story verbally.
instruction Instructions.
drift Plan.
blench Turn aside.
minister Dictate.
speeded Accomplished.

Act IV Scene 6

Mariana and Isabella discuss their forthcoming meeting with the Duke. Isabella would like to reveal the whole truth about Angelo, but, following the 'Friar's' instructions, she is content to leave the full revelation to Mariana.

Friar Peter comes to warn the girls of the Duke's approach.

Commentary

The rigidities of Isabella's morality, which were so apparent at the beginning of the play, are now only manifest in an uneasiness about not being able to tell the truth – on the 'Friar's' instructions. She is happy to accept that she is ruled by his advice. The audience is invited to share her perplexity over the instruction that the Duke may speak against her. Suspense reigns.

indirectly Equivocally.
loth Unwilling.
it i.e. speak indirectly.
peradventure Perchance.
the adverse side i.e. appearing to oppose her.
physic Medicine.
stand Position, a place to stand.
vantage i.e. an advantageous place in the assembly, from which she may present her petition.
generous Noble.
hent Taken up their positions.

Revision questions on Act IV

1 Show when and how the events of this act do not always work out as the Duke intended. How does he retrieve the situation in each case?

2 Are you able to justify the Duke's deviousness, or do you find some of what he does hard to stomach?

3 Discuss the relationship between Pompey and Abhorson in all its ramifications.

4 What is the significance of Barnardine with regard to the play as a whole?

5 How far are you able to sympathize with Angelo in Act IV Scene 4?

Act V Scene 1

The Duke is greeted near the city gates of Vienna by Escalus and Angelo. The final act of the drama is under way; what happens has been organized in advance by Vincentio in his 'Friar' guise. After the formalities of greeting, they are interrupted by the arrival of Isabella, who cries out against Angelo, demanding justice. The general conclusion is that she must be mad to level accusations of murder, hypocrisy and virgin-violation against so worthy a person as the Deputy. The Duke, to Angelo's satisfaction no doubt, affects not to believe her. However, Vincentio does 'admit' that she speaks logically, even though she is clearly demented. Isabella persists in her story, claiming that she was violated, and that Claudio was murdered, despite her 'giving in' to Angelo. Previously, she had expressed some uneasiness about having to maintain this fiction – but she plays her part well. She is supported in some of what she says by the intervention of Lucio, who persists in interrupting the proceedings – much to the Duke's annoyance. After she has told her story, Vincentio still pretends not to believe her and hands her over to an officer – she is to be taken to prison for slandering Angelo, whose 'good name' is, as yet, untarnished. Vincentio intimates that she must have been put up to these actions by someone who hates Angelo – and it is here that Friar Lodowick's name is mentioned – as a possible instigator of the plot to defame the Deputy. Lucio can vouch for the existence of this 'ghostly father', whom he proceeds to slander vehemently.

At this point, Friar Peter, who has been attending Isabella, comes to the fore: he professes to know Lodowick, and, contrary to the opinion expressed by Lucio, he knows him to be an honourable man. Peter believes that Angelo has been wronged by Isabella; he also suggests that Lodowick – at present suffering from a fever – will be able to clear Angelo's name. In the meantime, there is a witness who may be of help in the matter: enter Mariana, heavily veiled. She refuses to remove her veil, until she is bidden so to do by her husband. What she says at first appears enigmatic, but the substance of her claim is that Isabella cannot have had an assignation with Angelo, for at the alleged time, he was making love to her. Angelo demands that she remove her veil – and true to her vow, she does so. Confronted by the woman he spurned, Angelo is forced to admit that he knows her, but he is able to maintain his innocence upon the strength of his reputation. The Duke goes along with this, asserting that Mariana must be part of the confederacy which seeks to discredit Angelo. Friar Peter must be a party to it as well. The only solution would seem to be that Friar Lodowick be fetched. Accordingly, the Provost is dispatched to bring him to the proceedings. The Duke leaves, giving instructions that Escalus and Angelo should get to the bottom of the matter.

Escalus begins by asking Lucio what he knows of this mysterious Friar. Lucio slanders him. Isabella is summoned, but before she can be questioned, the process is interrupted by the arrival of the 'Friar' (in fact, of course, the Duke in disguise once more). Escalus demands to know why he has 'suborn'd' the women to slander Angelo, and to cast aspersions on the Duke – eventually he is threatened with the rack. The 'Friar's' assertions about the corruption in Vienna are not listened to. After he has had to endure some more insults, and just as he is about to be taken off to prison, the Duke is unmasked by his slanderer, Lucio. Immediately the Duke bails Isabella, Mariana and Friar Peter. Lucio is apprehended just as he is about to sneak off. Angelo is supplanted and the Duke begins to administer justice.

Straightaway, Angelo realizes that he has been discovered: he confesses and asks for the death sentence to be passed upon him. In reply, the Duke demands that he rights the wrong done to Mariana by marrying her. Vincentio next laments that he was not quick enough to prevent Claudio's execution, and he 'comforts' Isabella. Angelo returns with his new bride; Friar Peter has performed the ceremony. For his crimes Angelo is summarily sentenced to death. Immediately, Mariana launches upon an impassioned plea for her husband's life. Vincentio remains unmoved until Isabella joins Mariana in asking that Angelo should be spared. The argument is advanced that Angelo did not sin against her in deed, but only in thought. Suddenly, it occurs to the Duke that he has fault to find with the Provost: why was Claudio executed at such an unusual hour and without special warrant? The Provost admits that he did wrong, but defends himself by claiming that he acted upon some 'advice' that he was given – Barnardine can testify to this effect.

No sooner does Barnardine arrive than the Duke quits him of all his faults, and he is advised to lead a better life. In company with Barnardine is a 'muffled fellow', who, of course, turns out to be Claudio! The Duke proposes marriage to Isabella.

The way is now clear for the Duke to grant mercy to Angelo – he is instructed to love Mariana. The fate of Lucio remains undecided. How will the Duke requite him for all the insults which he has had to endure? Lucio's sentence is fitting: he must marry the whore whom he has got with child – the prospect does not please him.

Finally, Claudio is required to marry his Juliet, Escalus is given the hope of material reward and the Provost is to be offered promotion. The Duke exits, strongly hinting that he would like Isabella to marry him – provided, of course, that she gives her consent.

Commentary

The long and complicated final scene is the dénouement of the Duke's plotting. In a manner of speaking, it is a play within a play: the Duke has organized the 'drama' and directs the characters, although they, of course, do not at the time recognize his unseen hand at work. Only the Duke and we the audience are in full possession of the facts, which naturally gives rise to much dramatic irony.

In ringing tones, the Duke congratulates Angelo (and Escalus) on their good government of the city during his absence. Angelo accepts the credit, thereby unwittingly increasing the shame of his unmasking, when it comes. Isabella next plays her part: she maintains the fiction of her violation, demanding justice for the 'wrongs' which Angelo has done her. Of course, it is partly an act. Isabella's demand for justice is real enough, but her high-flown, rhetorical style gives rise to suspicion that she is uttering words that she has prepared, just as the Duke's measured enquiries as to the nature of her complaint against Angelo are designed to make the deputy feel the maximum of discomfort. Angelo's silence probably betokens guilt and anxiety – it would be up to the actor to convey this to the audience. Certainly Isabella's punctilious definition of the wrong she has suffered is tailor-made to impinge upon that part of Angelo's character which we have observed to be remorseful.

Suspense is further heightened by the arrival of the veiled Mariana. Shakespeare presents her interrogation comically, by means of jokes involving mistaken identity and double entendres. When she unveils, the shock to Angelo's equilibrium may easily be imagined – but he is able to maintain his balance (whilst admitting that he knows the girl) by clinging to the notion, already suggested by the Duke, that his accusers are agents of some 'mightier' person who has set them on. It is a notable moment of dramatic irony.

When the 'Friar' reappears he proceeds to denounce Angelo and the whole city. He is promptly seized upon and eventually his hood is wrenched off by Lucio. We may note here how the mood has changed abruptly: we are now in the world of low comedy. Yet a few moments earlier we were listening to the impassioned plea of Isabella. Here, as throughout the play, Shakespeare keeps careful control over an audience's reaction to what is being presented. The interweaving of the comedy with the serious elements in the play has prevented the moments of high drama from slipping over into tragedy. Equally, as so often in Shakespeare, the comic scenes are vehicles for some of his most serious ideas. It is somehow fittingly ironic that the moment that should represent the climax of the whole drama is handled with such lightness of touch, although I suppose that it is arguable that *the* climactic moment is the unmasking of Angelo. The two moments of revelation are neatly differentiated.

The Duke now assumes his proper place: the judgement seat. Angelo asks that his confession of guilt be heard and that he should suffer 'sequent death'. In an earlier phase of the play this would have been his handling of the situation. But it is not the Duke's. True to his design, which is to seek the ultimate reconciliation of all the parties, the Duke orders that Angelo should right the wrong done to Mariana and marry her. Once this has been achieved, he imposes the death sentence, and the stage is set for the granting of mercy. Before the operation of mercy, however, it is necessary that Mariana and Isabella should plead for Angelo's life. Significantly, the Duke is deaf to Mariana's pleadings; it is only when Isabella adds her voice in supplication for the man, whom she still believes to be responsible for her brother's death, that mercy is granted, and even then this must wait upon the pardon which is granted to Barnardine and the 'unmuffling' of Claudio. The fact that Claudio still lives means that no murder has been committed: the way is clear for the pardoning of Angelo. To unravel the precise significance of these events is not easy. We may begin by noting what has been achieved with Isabella: she has abandoned the harsh frigidities of her earlier life, she has admitted publicly to having been dishonoured, she has been disbelieved and arrested – yet despite all this she can be moved by the appeal of Mariana to plead for the man whom she has most reason to hate. Her plea is for justice, but it is couched in terms that seek to extenuate Angelo's faults, rather than a spirit of vengeance. It is to this act of Charity that the Duke responds. The fact that Isabella can plead for Angelo at all is a measure of the 'education' which she has received during the play.

Angelo's pardon is somewhat troubling. Surely, he does not 'deserve' it? Yet what would be gained by imposing some rigorous sentence upon him? Angelo has confessed, declared himself penitent and asked for the sentence of death to be passed upon him. He is thus ripe for the Duke to exercise the Divinely-inspired prerogative of mercy. This is a play imbued with the spirit of Christianity: we are reminded of Isabella's pleading to Angelo:

Why, all the souls that were, were forfeit once,
And He that might the vantage best have took
Found out the remedy.

The play ends with the comic judgement of Lucio, against whom the Duke may have something of a grudge! Again reconciliation is the presiding mood: Lucio is forced to marry the girl whom he has made pregnant, just as Claudio marries his Juliet. Only one question remains: does the Duke marry Isabella? Neatness and harmony would seem to suggest that they lived happily ever after. But Isabella never replies to the Duke's offer – and we are left to draw our own conclusions.

Forerunning more requital In anticipation of further reward.
bonds Obligations.
wards Cells, as in prison cells.
covert bosom Undisclosed affection.
forted Strengthened.
tooth of time Ravages of time.
razure Erasure (of forgetfulness).
outward courtesies . . . keep within A highly ironical remark in the light of what we know to be within Angelo.
Vail your regard Look down upon.
Here is Lord Angelo The Duke keeps up the pretence.
not truer It is as strange as it is true that his name is Angelo.
infirmity of sense i.e. she's mad.
conjure Call upon.
caitiff Rogue.
absolute Perfect.
dressings Trappings of authority.
caracts Signs of office.
forms Formalities.
frame Framework.
dependency . . . thing One matter follows logically from another.
inequality i.e. because I am socially inferior.
I wish you now then I wish that you would hold your peace now.
warrant Assure.
warrant The Duke puns with the meaning 'warrant for your arrest'.
pernicious Wicked.
Mended again It is now amended.
the needless process by Setting aside the inessentials.
refell'd Rejected.
concupiscible Sensual.
intemperate Ungovernable.
confutes Defeats.
fond Foolish.
suborn'd Bribed

it imports no reason It is utterly unreasonable.
vehemency Enthusiasm, vigour.
proper i.e. which he himself possesses.
weigh'd Judged.
by himself In the light of his own character.
set Inspired. Ironical: it was the Duke who has inspired Isabella to speak out in this way.
countenance i.e. the Duke appears to countenance (permit) such evils.
On him so near us i.e. Angelo.
practice Plotting.
ghostly (a) spiritual, and (b) literally ghost-like, insubstantial.
lay A layman.
retirement Absence.
swing'd Beaten.
saucy Impudent, shameless.
scurvy Vile.
abus'd Deceived.
touch Taint.
soil Evil.
vouches Asserts.
mere Personal.
probation Proof.
convented Called upon.
vulgarly Publicly.
punk Whore.
moe More.
abuse Deception.
the match Meeting.
supply Satisfy.
proportions Marriage-portion, dowry.
of composition Of what had been agreed.
levity Suggests moral laxity.
confixed Firmly fixed.
scope Freedom.
touch'd Injured.
informal Mad.
instruments Agents.
member i.e. of a plot.
Compact i.e. in collusion with (Isabella).
seal'd in approbation Confirmed with proof.
well-warranted Well-approved.
with Concerning.
Cucullus non facit monachum (Lat: 'A monk's hood does not make a monk'.) Proverbial, clearly ironical in view of the Duke's disguise.
enforce Emphasize.
privately An obscene pun.
darkly Secretly.
light (a) 'licentious' and (b) literally light in weight.

let the devil . . . throne Proverbial: 'even the devil is worthy of some respect'.
in us i.e. I represent the Duke.
retort Reject.
manifest Obviously just cause.
your trial . . . mouth Hand over the administration of justice to a villain.
of his proper ear And within his own hearing.
tax Accuse.
touse Rack.
provincial i.e. he is not subject to the local jurisdiction.
stew A pun on 'stew', meaning brothel.
forfeits . . . mark It was a custom of the time for barbers to post a joke-list of forfeits in their shops as punishments for mock crimes. Thus they were as much for mockery, as to be noticed seriously: 'marked'.
fleshmonger Lecher, pimp.
close Come to an agreement.
giglets Silly girls.
sheep-biting Sheep-biting dogs, synonymous with 'vicious criminal'.
three i.e. Isabella, Mariana and Friar Peter.
of him The Duke now assumes the place of Angelo.
office Service.
undiscernible Found out.
passes Trespasses.
session i.e. court session.
sequent With death to follow.
Advertising Taking due note of.
Attorney'd Acting in your interests.
vassal Subject.
unknown Unrecognized.
free Generous.
obscur'd Disguised.
rash remonstrance Blatant demonstration.
brain'd Destroyed.
That life, etc. Claudio enjoys a better life now that he is free from the fear of death, which haunted him in this life.
salt Lustful.
adjudg'd Condemned.
his proper tongue His own tongue. Justice personified here.
vantage The advantage of leniency.
instate and widow The Duke grants Mariana the widow's rights to Angelo's estate.
definitive i.e. my mind's made up.
importune Seek to persuade her to your cause.
paved bed Presumably Claudio was buried under the paving stones of the prison. It may refer to his tombstone.
moulded Created out of.

due Appropriate.
His act . . . intent He did not actually carry out the wicked deed which he intended.
buried . . . way i.e. let them be treated like bad intentions which never came to fruition.
Thoughts are no subjects You cannot punish a man merely for what he thinks. Intentions are merely thoughts, not deeds.
advice Consideration.
slip Fall.
grossly Mightily, blatantly.
squar'st Organizes (your life accordingly).
quit Exonerate.
quickening A new liveliness.
quits Pays you back.
her worth . . . yours She is equal to you in worth.
remission in myself The Duke is full of the spirit of forgiveness!
luxury Lust.
extol Praise. Used sarcastically, of course.
trick The usual practice around here.
pressing to death An extreme torture.
restore i.e. by marrying her. Claudio is ordered to marry Juliet.
confess'd her Acted as her confessor.
more gratulate Escalus is to be rewarded materially – with more than just thanks. 'Gratulate'=gratifying.
motion Proposal.
behind To come.

Revision questions on Act V

1 Outline, in note form, the main sequence of events in Act V.

2 Justify the timing of the Duke's revelation that Claudio is still alive.

3 Discuss the role of Mariana in this act.

4 What evidence from the text would lead you to the conclusion that the Duke is stage-managing the events of the act?

5 How appropriate do you find the Duke's treatment of Angelo?

6 What reasons might there be for Isabella refusing the Duke's offer of marriage?

7 How satisfying do you find the dénouement of the play?

Shakespeare's art in *Measure for Measure*

Setting

Although the play is set nominally in Vienna, it is obvious that Shakespeare really writes of a society which shares some of the features of his own. There is evidence to suggest that the validity, and the sinfulness or otherwise, of clandestine marriages was a live issue in Elizabethan England. Shakespeare himself contracted such a marriage.

It is maintained by some critics that the play was written with an eye to King James I. It is known, for example, that the King had a dislike of crowds and public show – a similar notion is expressed by the Duke. Perhaps even more significantly, James I was known to have a particular interest in the art of good government – he had written treatises on the topic. There are similarities of viewpoint between the King's *Basilikon Doron* and *Measure for Measure*.

Vienna and the world of the play

The city of Vienna is portrayed as a place of extremes, where opposites rub shoulders and discover remarkable correspondences. The sexual abstinence of Isabella is linked with the licentiousness of the brothel. Angelo straddles both worlds, appearing to advocate restraint whilst at the same time inwardly lusting after the nun. Lucio, too, links the aristocratic world and the dissolute world of Pompey and Mistress Overdone. Life teems and death abounds. We hear of the fertility of Juliet, who is about to give birth and we hear of the death sentence which faces her husband. The Duke speaks of death as something to be welcomed as a release from the trivialities and torments of life. Death is preferred to dishonour by Isabella. At the other end of the scale death is a matter of supreme indifference to Barnardine, whose only certainty is that he will not be put to death to suffer another's convenience. In the middle is Claudio, who is first brought to an acceptance of his own extinction, but later comes to express his abject terror at the possible torments that await him after he has crossed that 'bourn' from whence 'no traveller returns'.

The world of the play is also full of false appearances. A duke masquerades as a Friar; Mariana is a substitute bed-mate for Angelo; the Duke's return is in fact a carefully devised charade. Angelo's appearance of rectitude masks his inward nature, which at the beginning is concealed even from himself. The Duke believes himself to be immune from 'the dribbling dart of love': he is to learn otherwise when he falls in love with Isabella. Isabella herself learns that charity is a virtue which outshines chastity, and she abandons her appearance of chastity, in the furtherance of the Duke's schemes. Eventually, feeling the bond of human sympathy with Mariana, she pleads for the life of the man who wronged her, whereas formerly she had shown reluctance to plead for her condemned brother. One may suppose that she abandons the nun's habit and decides to live in the real world, although admittedly Shakespeare leaves this a somewhat open question.

From this multiplicity of human life certain ideas may become apparent, which seem to embody truths. First, people should prize self-knowledge. Self-deception is seen as deadly, cutting the self-deceived off from the life-enhancing virtues of mercy and charity. Secondly, a rigid adherence to principle at the expense of human feeling is shown to be destructive and may be itself a means by which people conceal from themselves their true natures and responsibilities to their fellow-men. Ironically, it is by means of a deception that the Duke exposes the truth of Angelo's vice and brings Isabella to a recognition of the supreme value of Christian charity. Thirdly, although the law in the hands of the corrupt ruler may seek to stamp out, by tyrannous means, human sexuality, in the end it is doomed to failure: this is a truth which Pompey expresses as he confronts the rigour of Angelo:

> Does your worship mean to geld and splay all
> the youth of the city?

Simply expressed, this means that you cannot make people good by passing laws against evil. The best that the law can hope to achieve is to curb man's anti-social tendencies so that they remain within the bounds of order, and even in this task the law will inevitably face certain failure. The Pompeys of this world are great survivors. Fourthly, we see embodied in Angelo the truth that 'power tends to corrupt and absolute power corrupts absolutely'. It is reasonable to suppose that had Angelo not been granted power then he would not have 'fallen'. But Isabella in seeking her brother's life, put herself in the power of Angelo, and the temptation to use it, purely in his own interests, and against his own avowed principles proved irresistible. Finally, in the management of this imperfect world such qualities as mercy, charity and human decency are necessary for survival and harmony.

Themes

Order

As the Duke himself admits, the city state of Vienna is in a parlous condition. After years of leniency, authority barely exists:

The baby beats the nurse, and quite athwart
Goes all decorum.

The law is 'more mocked than feared' and 'liberty plucks justice by the nose'. It is the God-given duty of the ruler to maintain order within the state; in this duty the Duke has clearly failed. The appointment of Angelo as Deputy is an attempt to retrieve the situation, and he is invested with the power of 'morality and mercy' in Vienna. Thus one of the central questions of the play is raised: given a breakdown in law and order, how may a ruler be expected to restore the sanctity of the law?

Angelo's response is to act immediately and with extreme severity; in particular he is harsh upon all forms of sexual indulgence, and in this respect he is acting upon a delicate area of human activity. The sexual drive is, of course, the most powerful of instincts, and it is both creative and destructive. Angelo's imposition of his authority, by means of the law, is indiscriminate. It is obviously necessary that prostitution and self-indulgence should be curbed by the framework of the law. Nobody would argue that Pompey should be imprisoned – the vice which his trade represents is disease-ridden and deathly: it threatens the harmony of the state. But Claudio is a different matter.

Authority

Claudio admits that he is culpable: he has committed fornication, and Juliet is with child. However, Angelo is wrong to equate him with Pompey. Indeed, in the eyes of Angelo's law, Claudio is being treated more harshly than the whoremonger and yet, self-evidently, his crime is much the less heinous. Claudio may be morally wrong in making love with Juliet before the Church has sanctioned their marriage, but they have undertaken marriage vows (albeit in secret) and their impulse is human and understandable. If Angelo has his way, the father will never know the child. Justice demands that Pompey goes to prison, and it demands, perhaps, that Claudio be rebuked for his crime, but it also requires, surely, that Claudio be allowed to live and to marry Juliet and bring up his offspring. In other words. in the name of common humanity, Angelo would be expected to exercise the prerogative of those put in authority by tempering justice with mercy.

Justice and mercy

In the case of Claudio the law is clearly involved with private morality. It was not in dispute at Shakespeare's time that the law had a right to concern itself with private behaviour, but the debate amongst philosophers of jurisprudence, as nowadays, was to what extent this concern should go. Tyrants would clearly wish to involve the law with all aspects of a citizen's behaviour, whereas ineffectual rulers would adopt a laissez-faire approach to such matters as private morality. Both extremes have spokesmen in *Measure for Measure*. Angelo is an absolutist: the law is the law and must be obeyed; the punishment for infringements of the law must be severe, or it will be held in contempt. Escalus, on the other hand, argues that all men are potentially guilty and therefore all criminals are deserving of sympathy, and ultimately, one supposes, of acquittal. Escalus, however, does not carry his theory into practice, for he does imprison Pompey on his second offence, having first dismissed him with a caution.

At the key moment of her plea before Angelo, Isabella also raises the issue of mercy. Angelo is first asked to show mercy to Claudio, whilst condemning his sin. This plea is easily overridden when Angelo points out that to pardon the man, in effect, is to sanction the crime. Next, Isabella reiterates the Escalus argument that Angelo himself might have 'slipped' had he been placed in similar circumstances to those of Claudio. This plea is ignored and we already know Angelo's views. Finally, Isabella pleads that Angelo should forgive the sinner after the manner of God, who sent His Son so that all sinful mankind might be redeemed. Asked to behave according to the example of Divine Mercy, Angelo can only reply that the law must be obeyed – he disclaims all personal involvement in the processes of law and punishment: 'It is the law, not I, condemn your brother.' There is a general validity in this principle and the wise ruler, acting with judicial authority, is entitled to make this claim. However, it evidently precludes the particular responsibility which should operate: the wise ruler also has within his power the exercise of mercy.

Realizing the futility of any further pleas, Isabella arrives at an overall denunciation of the right of one man to set himself up as a judge. 'Man, proud man' presuming to exercise authority over his fellow men is seen as a ridiculous figure and the object of Divine scorn, performing such tricks as make the Angels weep.

Authority – the Duke

In psychological terms the Duke has presented critics with problems, but if we set these aside and concentrate on his allegorical role in *Measure for Measure*, then his harmonizing aspect is clearly apparent. Throughout the play the Duke seems to be nudging the characters towards a deeper understanding of themselves and preparing them for the abandonment of fixed and irreconcilable positions. In the final act revelation is granted to both Isabella and Angelo.

At the beginning of Act V the Duke reappears, surrounded by the trappings of authority. In princely manner he greets Angelo and Escalus, promising to dispense 'favours'. These 'favours', which might be taken as related to Divine Grace, lead to the happy ending which has often been felt to be over-contrived and, in the case of Angelo, to be positively undeserved. However, we note that Angelo's pardon is dependent upon his recognition of his unworthiness to receive mercy. The scene opens with Isabella's plea for justice and Angelo's hiding behind his reputation for probity. This disguise can be maintained until the Duke is revealed. When this occurs, Angelo pronounces himself guilty, confesses and pleads for 'sequent death'. This he says is 'all the grace' he begs. The Duke responds by ordering his marriage, thus making Mariana an honest woman and legitimizing in the eyes of the world the consummation of their relationship in the walled garden.

Death still awaits him, until Isabella adds her plea for his reprieve; her argument, that in fact Angelo did not actually violate her, is important in worldly terms: a man should not be condemned for something he did not actually do. Thus Vincentio can now reprieve Angelo without undermining the right of the judge to exercise judgement: this would not have been so reasonable had not Angelo manifested his contrition publicly and had he actually made love to Isabella. As for Angelo's moral guilt, this is now a province for mercy, which the Duke unreservedly bestows. True, this is not felt to be 'measure for measure', but assuming the mantle of Divine Authority, the Duke is not concerned to judge Angelo as we, or the world, might judge him. All are guilty in the eyes of God, and from his position as God's deputy, Vincentio is possessed of the power to grant mercy to Angelo – the miserable, undeserving sinner.

Isabella is also forced during the play to abandon her entrenched position over her chastity. She has had to appear to consent to Angelo's wishes; she has persuaded Mariana to take part in the 'bed-trick', and she has had to make it appear (in public) that Angelo has violated her. And, furthermore, without knowing that her brother is still alive, she has found herself pleading for Angelo's life, rather than demanding revenge for her brother's life. All these actions, brought about through the agency of the Duke, represent a swallowing of her spiritual pride and involve the compromise of her previously held convictions. Her support for Mariana at the end is a triumph of charity, and opens the way for the operation of the Duke's grace towards his erring Deputy. Thus, rather than acting as a mouthpiece for arid principle, Isabella has been brought to a realization that she must live in the world – and even acknowledge the possibility of her own part in Angelo's fall:

I partly think
A due sincerity governed his deeds
Till he did look on me.

Finally, it is noteworthy that Pompey and Mistress Overdone do not partake of the Duke's forgiveness, for they are unrepentant sinners who are not fit vessels for ducal/Divine mercy. Reluctantly, too, in allegorical terms we can acknowledge a certain fitness in the diminished favour granted to Lucio. For all his attractions his slanderous tongue is an undermining of the authority upon which the harmony and good order of the state depends. No reasonable ruler could be seen to be over-tolerant of those who seek to diminish his authority by slanderous tittle-tattle.

Measure for measure

Judge not, that ye be not judged. For with what judgement ye judge, ye shall be judged: and with what measure ve mete, it shall be measured to you again (Matthew 7, 1–2).

The title of the play, derived from Christ's teaching in the Sermon on the Mount, is about the necessity for forgiveness. All men are sinners, we should all be prepared to acknowledge the beam in our own eye, before we cast out the mote in our brother's eye. The Old Testament teaches adherence to the law; Christ's teaching is about the spirit behind the law.

Angelo, as the law's representative, regards it as fitting that Claudio should pay the penalty for the act of fornication, which has left Juliet with child. He disregards the spirit of Christ's teaching which should call forth mercy and forgiveness – after all, Claudio is legally Juliet's husband, and has no intention of deserting her; they only lack the 'denunciation' of 'outward order'.

We learn in the course of the play of Angelo's unfitness to judge Claudio, because he himself contracted a similar marriage with Mariana – and his moral standing is more dubious because he deserted her. Furthermore, Angelo is driven by a secret lust for a nun. In making love with Mariana, Angelo commits the same offence as Claudio.

According to the law of the Old Testament ('an eye for an eye . . .') Angelo should die: retributive justice cries out for it. The Duke makes this very point:

An Angelo for Claudio; death for death.
Haste still pays haste, and leisure answers leisure;
Like doth quit like, and Measure still for Measure.

Angelo himself calls for his own death.

But the healing spirit of Christian forgiveness now begins to work. Angelo expresses remorse, confesses and repents his sins. Mariana (an agent for the forces for mercy in the play) begs for her husband's life and she is joined by Isabella (who has no cause to seek Angelo's salvation). The Duke, at first, is unmoved by these pleadings but he eventually pardons Angelo and the play ends on a note of reconciliation and looks forward to future harmony.

Thus the play is a critique of the retributive idea of justice: measure can only truly be said to answer measure, if human justice, administered by fallible human beings, is tempered by a spirit of Christian forgiveness. If the circumstances allow – and they do in Angelo's case, as they did for Claudio – then reason and the teaching of Christ demand the exercise of mercy.

The characters

The Duke

a looker-on here in Vienna

The Duke's decision to put the government of Vienna in the hands of Angelo is a response to his own sense of failure. The laws are ignored and corruption is prevalent. His concomitant decision to return, disguised as the Friar, indicates that he has not abrogated his responsibilities: such a trick may be regarded as an approved 'modus operandi' for a ruler. Throughout Angelo's tenure of office, the presence of the Duke, albeit disguised, provides the audience with the reassurance that the tragic potential of events will not be realized. The Duke's motives for appearing to quit his city are clearly stated: Angelo is to sweep the city clean of corruption (the result of ducal leniency); the odium necessarily part of such a moral crusade will attach itself to Angelo, thus presumably enabling the Duke to begin again with 'a clean slate'. The assumption of a disguise will enable him to observe this process in action. It will also give him an opportunity to test the true worth of Angelo: 'Hence shall we see,/If power change purpose, what our seemers be.'

In his role as Friar, the Duke may be seen as an allegorical figure, akin to Divine Providence. As the play unfolds, he finds himself unable to sustain his role as a mere observer and purveyor of spiritual comfort; he becomes increasingly interventionist, so that after Act III, Scene 1, we find that his time is spent largely in organizing the other characters to a realization of themselves and bringing about a happy, harmonious ending.

However, the notion that the Duke is Divine Providence will not quite do: sometimes he is shown not to be in control of events, as, for example, when Angelo decides to have Claudio executed despite Isabella's apparent acquiescence in his lust.

If we retain this idea that the Duke is a consciously redemptive force in the play, then it is possible to see the 'justification' in allegorical terms for some of the 'difficult' aspects of his behaviour: his tendency to 'use' people and his delay in permitting Isabella the knowledge that her brother has not been executed, for example.

At times Vincentio enunciates some of the larger issues which are raised by the play. In this context we may note his comments on law and order which he makes to Friar Thomas (I, 3), his speech to Claudio beginning 'Be absolute for death' and his sententious utterances at the end of Act III. All these 'statements', which seem to stand out from the surrounding text, confirm the Duke's role as a choric commentator or contributor to the 'debate' element in the play.

But what of the Duke as a personality? It is possible to argue that he has a role in the drama (providential, structural – as an initiator and stage manager of the plot and choric), but he remains somewhat shadowy as a man. Lucio describes him as 'the old, fantastical Duke of dark corners', and we may agree that there is sometimes something rather ludicrous about this 'meddling friar'. Escalus pays him an unreserved tribute when he describes him as 'One that, above all other strifes, contended especially to know himself . . . Rather rejoicing to see another merry than merry at anything which professed to make him rejoice: a gentleman of all temperance.' Yet, the Duke's most 'human' moments seem to be when he is expressing his irritation with the barbs of Lucio. It is true that he does seem to revel in his scheming – sometimes with near disastrous results.

We have mentioned that some of the Duke's behaviour seems morally dubious. It is perhaps fair to mention that it is possible to give a very adverse reading of his character. There are some awkward questions about the Duke which need to be faced. Is he justified in leaving the state in the hands of Angelo – whose past history is known to him and yet on whom he heaps so much praise in the first scene? His consolation of Isabella and Claudio seems, from one point of view, singularly inept and lacking in human sympathy: he indulges in heavy-handed moralizing, rather than displaying human warmth. How can he, with a clear conscience, instigate the bed-trick with Mariana, when he has condemned Claudio's bedding with Juliet? In this instance, he covers up the moral dubiety with disconcerting smoothness:

To bring you (i.e. Mariana and Angelo) thus together, 'tis no sin,
Sith that the justice of your title to him
Doth flourish the deceit.

This hardly squares with his words to Juliet in Act II Scene 3. The Duke's attitude towards Barnardine is frankly callous, and we can only delight in Barnardine's refusal to co-operate. Also, his treatment of Lucio at the end of the play (in a sense, he is the only character to suffer) leads to the inescapable conclusion that the Duke is motivated by a desire to settle a grudge. Lucio has been the only person to express less than admiration for Vincentio.

Thus it is possible to arrive at an interpretation of the Duke's character which is far from flattering. The beneficient, providential reconciler becomes a puritanical, evasive, manipulator, who subordinates human beings and their feelings to his own vision of how the world should be. This would be a world in which music is suspect, for it may through its charm 'make bad good, and good provoke to harm'. It would be a world in which compassion would be in short supply; in its stead arid moral precepts would abound. During the final scene, this well-intentioned but small-minded man presides over the working out of his schemes and passes the whole charade off as the manifestation of his justice and mercy. At last, Claudio is permitted to marry his Juliet – in other words, he conforms. Barnardine receives a pardon and a moral injunction. Blatantly unsuited couples are married off (Angelo/Mariana, Lucio/Kate). Isabella receives the offer of the ducal hand in marriage. It's a very smooth, well-timed performance – but in order that it may be achieved, too many characters have been forced to sacrifice the discordant, important parts of themselves which have brought them to life in the first half of the play. The whole thing is so unreal that it might be termed a parody of the operation of justice and mercy.

The way in which we interpret the Duke's character can thus radically affect the interpretation of the play. Admirers of the Duke will see it as a sort of parable, and stress the allegorical mechanistic features of his role – his faults (and they do exist) will be indulged and explained as the foibles of a fallible ruler. The Duke's detractors will see the play's overt message as being contradicted, once an attempt is made to incorporate his 'faults' into a consistent interpretation of his character.

Isabella

The hand that hath made you fair hath made you good

Isabella is a postulant: she has taken the preliminary vows demanded by that strictest of orders, the Poor Clares. Even so, she wishes that 'more restraint' were being asked of her. When she is first acquainted with her brother's sin by Lucio, her first reaction is that Claudio must marry the girl. On hearing of Angelo's rigour, she first professes a feeling of inadequacy before the task of pleading for her brother's life. But she agrees to see what she can do. It is here that the difficulties begin. The puritan in her nature makes it apparent that she is acting as an advocate rather than a sister. Lucio rebukes her for the coldness of her approach. Isabella's problem is that she shares Angelo's view of morality; she is unhappy that she is being asked, in effect, to condone the sin in seeking her brother's reprieve. Her next appeal, based on the grounds that he who is without sin should cast the first stone, touches Angelo on a raw nerve – he is already beginning to feel the power of her sexual attraction.

Matters come to a head in her next interview with Angelo, when, after some preliminary skirmishing on the theme of mercy, she is presented with the possibility of saving Claudio at the expense of her chastity. There is no escape from her predicament: Angelo, by virtue of his reputation, is untouchable – her 'proclamation' of his wickedness simply would not be believed. She makes her choice: 'More than our brother is our chastity.' There is much that might be said against this dictum. Chastity is a state of mind rather than a physical condition – the implication here is that Isabella might yield and still remain spiritually inviolate since an enforced sin is arguably no sin at all. A man's life is at stake. Isabella has had to face these arguments (at the time posed hypothetically) from Angelo. Now that she faces them in reality, she does not falter in her resolve. As a postulant, to break her vow on any level would put her immortal soul at risk. Better that Claudio should die, than that she should suffer an eternity in hell. It is not possible to resolve this argument, and how we react will determine our attitude towards Isabella. Some will see her as prudish, essentially frightened of the physical fact of sex. In defence of her honour, she is inconsistent: much of her argument with Angelo stressed the mercy of God, yet she seems unable to conceive that God might show her sin any mercy. She seems to imagine that God is as legalistic as Angelo. An alternative view of Isabella is to see her as a symbol of purity, courageously refusing to compromise herself and her immortal soul by taking the decision which would save her brother's life.

There are some important considerations which, in fairness, need to be made. First, in Isabella's defence, for what may be an admittedly unpopular stance, it should be remembered that she is a young woman who is forced to face her dilemma in an entirely frightening and inhospitable situation. She seeks the retirement of a nunnery, but she is persuaded out of her chosen environment to face the lustful, yet arid Angelo. She has no person to turn to (the Friar has not yet materialized) and thus perhaps we can sympathize with her clinging to the certainty of her chastity – in a confused and confusing world it seems a very human reaction. Secondly, if we allow Isabella the validity of her theological position with regard to chastity, we should perhaps nonetheless question the manner in which she turns on her brother in his need. In brief, she strikes many critics as far too strident. It should be possible to hold on to her convictions and still show a modicum of human understanding of Claudio's desperation. ' 'Tis best thou diest quickly' seems horribly cruel, and does not her ringing denunciation of Claudio's dishonesty and cowardice betoken her own spiritual pride?

Whether we like her or not, we cannot but be engaged by Shakespeare's creation. She is a woman of conviction, intelligence and spirit. Once the Friar/Duke gets to work with her, she seems to suffer a diminution. It is possible, in terms of the play's allegory, to see the necessity for her learning the hard lesson of spiritual humility. The absolutism, which she shares with Angelo, has to be tempered by a recognition that even she has no claim to be at one with the angels. The Duke's plans for her force her to compromise some of her dearly-held beliefs: she has to go before Angelo, swallow her pride, and appear to agree to his desires – and she has to maintain this charade in public, a bitter lesson for someone who has held her honour so dear. She has to persuade Mariana to undertake the 'bed-trick'. In the final scene, in response to Mariana's need, she bows the knee and pleads for her persecutor's life. It is not so much that her protest at such 'requirements' seems muted, but more that one finds her seeking Angelo's reprieve upon such intellectually feeble, if legal, grounds: 'His act did not o'ertake his bad intent, And must be buried but as an intent/That perished on the way.' The Isabella of the first part of the play, one feels, would have done better than this.

Angelo

man . . . dressed in a little brief authority

Angelo is a Puritan: his appearance of moral rectitude, his humourlessness and his distaste for pleasure are all unmistakable indicators of the puritanical attitude to life. Granted absolute power in Vienna, Angelo sets about his task of cleaning up the city by demolishing its brothels and reinstituting the death penalty for fornication. It is clearly time that Mistress Overdone, Pompey and their kind were called to account, but

Angelo's treatment of Claudio oversteps the bounds of due moderation. The new deputy is a stickler for the law, and he is deaf to the appeals of the Provost and Escalus.

Angelo had asked the Duke for some test of his virtue to be made before he was given authority; this test arrives in the shape of Isabella, who comes to seek mercy for her brother. Angelo uses his power to coerce the girl into his bed. He is captivated not only by her beauty, but also he is irresistibly entranced by her purity of spirit. The psychology is apt here: the Puritan falls foul of the sin which he abominates in others. Before the appearance of Isabella, Angelo presented to the world an impression of rock solid probity – only the most observant might have noticed a curtness of manner and impatience which betrayed the underlying innner tensions of the man. In fact, of course, Angelo has never been a saint. As the Duke knew, before he appointed him Deputy, Angelo had already deserted the hapless Mariana because her dowry did not materialize. He is basically a cruel, unfeeling man. On losing patience with Froth, Elbow and Pompey he storms out of the court, hoping that Escalus will find 'good cause to whip them all'. Again, when he realizes that Isabella will not accede to his wishes, he threatens to torture Claudio before putting him to death. His treatment of Juliet is devoid of human pity.

In common with many Puritans, Angelo regards himself as a repository of saintliness. When he feels his desire for Isabella mounting within him, the self-loathing, which is often a component of rigid Puritanism, becomes very apparent:

What is't I dream on?
O cunning enemy that, to catch a saint,
With saints dost bait thy hook.

Just as his shallow legalism was unable to comprehend the demands of common humanity, so his rigidly held moral beliefs quickly crumble once they are assailed by the promptings of 'sharp appetite'. A divided man, Angelo is an interesting character. But Shakespeare does not really go on to explore Angelo's inner nature, and we find that we are asked to concentrate upon his villainy. As a Machiavel Angelo is an effective portrayal; we see him employing a devilish cunning to exercise his will over Isabella, but in so doing he is answering the demands of the plot – the complexities of his character at which Shakespeare had hinted earlier in the play disappear. Indeed, Angelo himself disappears from our view for the whole of Act III and all but the final 'business' scene of Act IV.

When Angelo is summoned to meet the Duke (Act V) we know that he is to be called to judgement. He successfully hides behind the 'outward-saintedness' of his reputation, despite the revelations of Isabella and Mariana. He does not confess until the Duke is finally unmasked by Lucio. Once he realizes the pretence of innocence can no longer be maintained, he demands that the death penalty be imposed upon him so perhaps earning our sympathy. In response to the pleas of Mariana (his new wife) and Isabella ('I partly think/A due sincerity governed his deeds/ Till he did look on me'), Angelo is granted mercy. It is all rather unsatisfactory, in that one feels that he has been let off too lightly. True, he has been brought to confession and repentance – and if the play's ending is regarded in the spirit of the Romantic Comedies, then perhaps we should not ask for more: in the interests of all-round harmony and good cheer the forgiving words of the Duke may be accepted as adequate to the occasion:

Well, Angelo, your evil quits you well.
Look that you love your wife, her worth worth yours.

However, it is also possible that we feel disappointed at such a dismissal and marrying-off of a character whose evil we have been asked to take seriously in the earlier part of the play.

Claudio

the most gentle Claudio

We first encounter Claudio as a victim of Angelo's harsh regime: he is under sentence of death. Oddly enough, he does not appear to question the justice of his treatment. The sentence is legal and the result of indulgence in the sin of 'thirsty evil' i.e. sexual indulgence. It is clear, however, that Shakespeare intends that we should regard him as a sympathetic character, not only because Lucio, Escalus, the Provost and Isabella are prepared to take his side, but also because his severe sentence is inappropriate to the crime. The clandestine marriage which he undertook with Juliet may properly be regarded as fitting him for the mercy of the beneficent ruler. Angelo, however, is neither humane nor reasonable; the reality of the sentence initiates the plot of the play.

Claudio's reaction to his imminent execution makes him a person with whom we can readily identify. He is comforted by the Duke/Friar after the 'Be absolute for death' speech, but it is soon apparent that hope for a reprieve has not been extinguished. When Isabella tells him of Angelo's proposal, he wavers: at first he is outraged at the assault upon his sister's honour, but as soon as it dawns upon him that there is a way of escape, he embraces it. Claudio's words 'Ay, but to die . . .' represent the 'answer' to the Duke's earlier speech which stressed the folly of clinging to life. In his sensuous apprehension of what it means to be a warm, living being, Claudio speaks as a sort of Everyman as he faces the prospect of his own mortality. The absoluteness of Isabella's condemnation of her brother's feelings ironically links her with Angelo. Claudio's remorse 'Let me ask my sister pardon. I am so out of love with life that I will sue to be rid of it.' further heightens our sympathy for him.

Shakespeare thus portrays Claudio as an essentially good-natured young man, trapped by warm and natural feelings towards the girl to whom he is betrothed, so that he must face the prospect of his own extinction. He does not wish to see his sister dishonoured in the cause of his salvation, but his desperate fear as he faces execution strikes a common chord in us all.

Lucio

Thou art the first knave that e'er mad'st a duke

Lucio is dissolute. He consorts with prostitutes, discusses his sexual predilections with coarse abandon, and is clearly associated with the forces for disorder. Yet he is one of the most attractive and enjoyable characters in the play. Whilst we cannot sympathize with his licentiousness, he earns our respect and liking because of his common decency. Lucio is entrusted with the task of conveying Claudio's message to Isabella: he carries out this responsibility in the name of friendship. His manner towards Isabella is teasing but respectful – he is totally out of sympathy with her vocation but he recognizes the goodness of the woman to whom he speaks. When Isabella meets Angelo, Lucio's encouragement melts the coldness of her plea – a fact which leads her into difficulties with Angelo.

Another attractive feature of Lucio is that he makes some good jokes, and we particularly enjoy his needling of the pompous Duke. Perhaps the price he pays for this – he is forced to marry his whore – is too high.

Lucio moves easily between the world of the high-born and the world of the whorehouse, but he is not disposed to confuse the two. He recognizes Pompey for what he is and refuses to bail him out of prison. Of course, Lucio stands as utterly opposed to

Angelo, and one appreciates the worldly wisdom expressed in the lines 'Yes, in good sooth, the vice is of a great kindred. It is well allied, but it is impossible to extirp it quite, friar, till eating and drinking be put down.' Lucio would also seem to be opposed to Claudio's view that human sexuality is potentially destructive. For Lucio sexual relations are part of the natural process, and as such should be pursued with the utmost vigour and lack of inhibition.

Escalus

Thanks, good friend Escalus, for thy much goodness

Escalus, with his long experience and wisdom, represents moderation in the admiration of judgement, whereas Angelo represents excess. Escalus seeks to mitigate the severity of the sentence passed upon Claudio and speaks for humane values rather than legalistic rigour: he advocates mercy, arguing that in similar circumstances Angelo himself might have fallen foul of the law. His argument is to no avail. When he is left to deal with Pompey's offence, Escalus pursues a patient investigation of the evidence and eventually dismisses the offender with a strong caution that he should mend his ways. When Pompey offends again, then Escalus has no hesitation in committing him to prison. Escalus may counsel moderation but he is also concerned to uphold the law.

Escalus, in his essentially humane attitude to the people with whom he has dealings, is a yardstick against which Angelo may be measured, but it can also be said that he represents a view of justice which may finally be inadequate. His criterion that we are all actual or potential sinners, and therefore have no right to judge others, may work in terms of personal relationships; however, it is questionable that such a philosophy should govern the administration of public affairs.

Mariana

There, at the moated grange, resides this dejected Mariana

Mariana obviously has an important role in the plot as the substitute for Isabella in the walled garden, thus making possible the Friar's 'bed-trick'. In former times, Angelo had rejected her partly on the grounds of her 'levity' – an unflattering description – but she strikes us as a romantic and attractive woman, as she listens to melancholy love-songs in her 'moated grange'. She remains faithful to Angelo, despite her harsh treatment at his hands, and she pleads ardently for his life before the Duke.

Minor characters

The Provost shows us the law with a human face: he is naturally unhappy with Claudio's sentence, and his concern for the welfare of the 'groaning Juliet' is wholly admirable. He performs his duties under Angelo with obvious reluctance; his overriding loyalty is to the Duke, and he willingly goes along with the Friar's plans on being convinced that they carry the Duke's authority. He is promised promotion at the end of the play.

Pompey, the bawd, is irredeemably licentious, insolent and given over to self-interest. His comic impact on the play is considerable and his refusal to be cowed by the repressive laws of Angelo put him firmly on the side of life rather than aridity. His refusal, too, to take judicial proceedings seriously, provides a comic counterweight to the potentially tragic consequences of the law when it is applied to Claudio. To save himself from a full term of imprisonment and a whipping Pompey is quite happy to act as Abhorson's assistant: bawd and hangman – both cater to the needs of unregenerate humanity; it is oddly appropriate that they come together.

Mistress Overdone, despite her profession of brothel-keeper, endears herself to us by her bustling, lively good nature. She is not much individualized, but she shows a human warmth towards Kate Keepdown, who has borne Lucio's child, and she seems genuinely concerned over Claudio's misfortunes.

Barnardine is the archetypal lovable villain. Hardened sinner he may be, but he earns our applause by his refusal to be executed simply because he does not feel 'fitted for it'. The Duke is forced to acknowledge defeat and pronounces him 'unfit to live or die'. Unlike Claudio, who also does not want to die, he refuses to be reconciled to his fate. Thus, Barnardine represents, at its lowest level, the unquenchable life-force.

Elbow is the comic constable, who gets his words all wrong. He is incompetent, hilarious and very well-meaning. The comedy here obviously contributes to a lightening of mood in the play.

Structure

The overall movement of the drama is from discord to harmony. The formality of the opening scene soon dissolves and we sense the corruption which the Duke's apparent departure is intended to rectify. The imposition of order by means of the strict application of law is shown to be flawed, not least because the legislator himself is a corrupt and divided man. The Duke, however, although in disguise, is a central figure and provides a focus of interest by means of which the audience remains in touch with the harmonizing motif in the play.

The final scene contrasts and parallels the opening of the play. It too begins on a formal note, involving the commissioning of Angelo, (this time to investigate the 'slanders' against him) and the apparent withdrawal of the Duke, who reappears as the Friar. But the outcome of the sequence is different and the play ends with marriage, mercy and harmony rather than fornication, violation, ruthless legalism and discord – the keynotes of the opening sequence.

Echoes and contrasts abound in the play – suggested by the title – for both Angelo and Claudio have contracted secret marriages, but contrastingly Claudio wishes to marry Juliet, whereas Angelo has deserted Mariana. Mariana and Isabella both plead for the lives of men whom they love: Mariana pleads for the husband who has wronged her, Isabella pleads for the brother whom she thinks has sinned. Angelo is a great sinner, Claudio is a minor sinner. Claudio deserves mercy from Angelo, but receives none; Angelo does not deserve mercy but receives it from the Duke. Ironies are forced on the reader's attention because of these parallels and contrasts; they also invite us to make judgements.

Within the play itself various ideas and themes are balanced. Claudio switches from an acceptance of death, urged on him by the Duke, to a heartfelt desire for life. Barnardine is indifferent to the fact of human extinction, but shares with Claudio the right to care about when it should be visited upon him. Isabella's rigid adherence to chastity is contrasted with the licence implicit in the life of Lucio. And this chastity is itself balanced by a corresponding need to show charity. Court and brothel, superficially antagonistic, are shown to be linked in corruption. Pompey is the servant of both. Constantly the audience is being asked to measure one idea against another.

In this play of extremes, it is perhaps not surprising that characters lack an overall consistency. Isabella clings to chastity, yet the providential harmonizing movement of the play requires that she participates in a plot which involves Mariana committing the very sin which she abhorred in her brother.

At times one feels that the psychological conviction of some of the writing sits very uneasily with the symbolic, folklore element in the tale. Thus Angelo's fevered recognition of the demon within himself, which is particularly vivid and convincing, fizzles out: Angelo, having been established as an interesting character, virtually disappears from the play until the final scene, when he re-emerges to accept without demur a marriage which is forced upon him. Indeed, with the exception of Claudio and Juliet, the marriages which form the 'traditional' ending of romance plays seem unsatisfactory, to say the least. Isabella does not even reply to the Duke's offer of his hand in marriage. Structurally speaking, symbolism and psychological truth to life are not easy bedfellows.

Style

Verse

Measure for Measure is not chiefly memorable for the glories of its poetry, but the play nonetheless reveals Shakespeare to be a master of dramatic blank verse. Shakespeare's handling of his medium is controlled and assured: it can convey ideas, sustain narrative, denote character, give expression to feelings and set mood – all in a vigorous and vivid manner.

The play opens with the Duke speaking in a formal manner:

Of government the properties to unfold
Would seem in me t' affect speech and discourse . . .

The rhythm here is stately, regular; the clauses carefully balanced. The effect is to give the impression of a contrived speech. The responses of Escalus and Angelo retain the dignity of the occasion. The characters of the speakers are apparent in some of the things they say, but Shakespeare is chiefly concerned to give a clear exposition of the Duke's resignation of power. In the second scene, when Claudio and Lucio speak, the effect is altogether more colloquial and the rhythms more akin to those of everyday speech – and there is no sense of awkwardness as we slip from verse to prose. Angelo, whilst he remains in control of himself, speaks with a measured fluency, but once he finds himself susceptible to Isabella his self-control evaporates, and this is captured in the staccato, faltering rhythm of his soliloquy:

What's this? What's this? Is this her fault, or mine?
The tempter, or the tempted, who sins most, ha? (II, 2, 163–4)

The rhythm conveys the deterioration of Angelo's personality. The overall effect is particularly heightened when the rhythm here is contrasted with the formality of the 'debate' between Isabella and Angelo which preceded it. Similarly, from a rhythmic point of view, it is instructive to compare the heavily-accented and end-stopped manner of the Duke's 'consolatory' speech about death with the fluid, dream-like quality which is evident in Claudio's contemplation of the possible horrors which may await him after death. Such examples could be multiplied. In general terms, Shakespeare's rhythms evoke a particular emotional response in the audience and indicate the emotional state of the speaker. They provide an important clue to the actor as to how a speech should be delivered, and are an effective means of keeping an audience alert to the shifting moods of the play.

Imagery

Shakespeare's imagery is also an important focus of interest. On a simple level, images are a means whereby thoughts and feelings may be given concrete form. The Duke's description of the anarchic state of his city is given great vividness by means of the word-pictures which are employed:

We have strict statutes and most biting laws,
The needful bits and curbs to headstrong weeds,
. . .
The baby beats the nurse, and quite athwart
Goes all decorum.

The idea conveyed here is simply that Vienna has become a topsy-turvy society: disorder reigns, laws are disregarded. The speech is structured in so far as it presents a catalogue of images of disorder. But along with the vividness goes variety: each verbal picture has something to contribute, none are redundant. The opening lines reveal that the Duke conceives of himself as a rider who has lost control of his mount, but they also have a symbolic import in that the image of the rider seeking to control an unruly horse represents man seeking to control wayward instincts – an idea which obviously has wide implications in the play as a whole: Isabella, Claudio and especially Angelo all have difficulty in controlling themselves. The metaphor thus has a frame of reference outside the merely political sphere of which the Duke ostensibly speaks. In this speech, too, the images which refer to the unruly young have an additional interest and illustrate how Shakespeare's word-pictures have an evocative power, which releases an audience's imagination. What are we to make of them? Of course, they can be taken simply as vivid realizations of disorder and the Duke, as a man, can be 'detached' from them and be regarded simply as adopting a choric role. But if we assume them to be a reflection of his character, we can ask ourselves what sort of man it is who would choose such images to describe disorder. Seen in this light they perhaps reveal the psychology of the bully who assumes the natural function of the father to be the birch and the proper role of the nurse to be to beat the baby. It is the psychological world of the sadist, devoid of love. This interpretation, linked with the notion that the Duke is the bossy friar, could provide an insight into his character. Obviously there are dangers in such an approach, but powerful imagery can often release such thoughts in the minds of critics and theatrical producers!

It is often a fruitful field of study to observe the images which recur in a play. *Measure for Measure*, for example, examines the subject of human sexuality. The corruption of Vienna is seen explicity in sexual terms: licence is seen to produce disease and there are frequent comic references to venereal infection which underline the deathly consequences of promiscuity. Claudio's impregnation of Juliet is seen by Lucio as part of nature's creative purpose, bringing about 'teeming foison'; however, sex involves appetite and pleasure – Claudio and Juliet have embraced prematurely. The result is that in giving way to appetite ('As those that feed grow full') Claudio has incurred deathly consequences. Thus far, sex is associated in terms of the imagery with fruitfulness, pleasure, death and disease. Angelo goes further: to him sexual indulgence is one of man's 'filthy vices' and this leads him to associate sexual desire with murder; the begetting of bastards is analogous to stamping the king's image on a false coin:

It were as good
To pardon him that hath from nature stolen
A man already made, as to remit
Their saucy sweetness that do coin heaven's image
In stamps that are forbid. 'Tis all as easy
Falsely to take away a life true made,
As to put mettle in restrained means
To make a false one.

Ironically, the 'coining' image here links Angelo with Pompey – both have a distinctly monetary view of the sexual 'transaction'.

A consideration of Shakespeare's choice of words will reveal that the play contains an unusual number of abstract nouns: 'authority', 'justice', 'mercy', 'grace', 'liberty', etc. As critics have pointed out these words indicate the central preoccupations of the drama and demonstrate that *Measure for Measure* is essentially a play of ideas.

Prose

Pompey and the other members of the lower orders of society

speak in prose. It is the language of the brothel: coarseness and lewd jokes hardly suit the medium of verse! Lucio often speaks in prose, too, as befits the gallant who frequents the baser reaches of society, although it is noteworthy that when he pays Isabella a visit in the nunnery, he slips into verse – as decorum demands. But prose is often spoken by the Duke, especially in those moments which require the unfolding of information and the prosecution of his schemes. Obviously, prose generates a lower emotional temperature than verse, and the fact that so much of the play is written in prose after the opening of Act III, has led some critics to believe that Shakespeare's interest and inspiration flagged during the second half of the play. This view should not be taken to imply that Shakespeare wrote bad prose. On the contrary, it could be argued that much of the Duke's prose is exceptionally good: he speaks in carefully controlled sentences, which are models of exposition and embellished with neat, felicitous phraseology.

Irony in *Measure for Measure*

Irony abounds in the play. As we look back over the happenings in the drama, the most unexpected reversals and correspondences come to light. Destiny seems to force the characters into behaving in ways which they could never have predicted. For example, one of the prime ironies in the play is that the chaste Isabella, who in Act II vehemently rejects the proposals of Angelo, and is prepared to see her relatively innocent brother die, by the end of the play falls to her knees to plead for the Deputy's life. Incidentally, by this time Angelo has himself changed from being her predator to becoming her victim. Again, it is similarly ironic that Angelo finds himself subject to the very lusts which he seeks to stamp out in others; the agent of this revelation is the saintliness in Isabella. Angelo perceives the irony of his situation:

O cunning enemy that, to catch a saint,
With saints dost bait thy hook. Most dangerous
Is that temptation that doth goad us on
To sin in loving virtue.

The Duke believes that he is impervious to the 'dribbling dart of love' but discovers that he has fallen in love with Isabella by the end of the play. He assumes the disguise of a friar in order to discover the truth about 'seemers'; he divests himself of the trappings of authority, in order to exert it more effectively. Both the Duke and Isabella perpetrate deception when they send Mariana to Angelo's embrace, which, in another context, would seem more appropriate to Pompey. Duke and nun become, in effect, pandars!

The impression created by these reversals of expectations is that the characters are in the grip of a destiny which forces them to re-evaluate themselves and their behaviour.

General questions

1 Explore the theme of 'justice' in *Measure for Measure.*

Note form suggested answer

Introduction
Theme apparent from Duke's remarks in I, 1.
Angelo given powers of 'mortality and mercy'.
Duke aware of effects of his leniency – I, 3.
Angelo's re-enactment of defunct statutes.

Angelo
Justice=ruthless repression. Does Claudio deserve the death penalty? It is the law, but is it *just*?

Important issue raised: Claudio condemned on legal grounds; admits his 'guilt'. But how far should the restraints of law impinge upon a man's natural appetites – in this case, sexuality? It is in the nature of law that it comes into conflict with the natural inclinations of man. *Thus* Angelo's 'curbing' of Claudio is a test case. Clearly we are meant to believe that Angelo has gone too far. Prostitution rightly curbed. Pompey and his world=disorder and disease.

Isabella
Like Angelo, condemns Claudio's sin.
Reluctantly pleads for pity.
Faced with the reality of human desires, she has decided on withdrawal from the world.

Isabella and Angelo
Both think that they have the answer to passion: Angelo believes that he has conquered it in himself and that he therefore has the right to repress it in others; Isabella thinks that she can turn her back on it.
Ironically, they contribute to each other's enlightenment. Angelo is forced to confront his own appetite – lust for Isabella. Isabella comes to learn that she must temper her principles with human kindness – which she does not show to Claudio.
N.B. II, 2 and II, 4 – Angelo facing the reality of his own nature.

Isabella faced with two claims: chastity/brother's life.
Angelo's evil brings the issue to the fore. What is wrong about Isabella is the *way* in which she holds fast to chastity: 'More than our brother is our chastity.' Spiritual pride? Where is human understanding for Claudio? Heartless holiness?

The Duke
Authority figure. Disguise enables observation of people and role of behind the scenes reconciler.
Comes into contact with all echelons of his society – and their attitudes – seeks to harmonize them.
N.B. Isabella's acquisition of pity (pleading on behalf of Mariana) – How is it brought about?

Justice and mercy
Angelo forced to make public aknowledgement of his own sinfulness.
He expresses repentance and asks to be judged by the criterion which he employed against Claudio. The Deputy expresses his common bond with the rest of sinful mankind. Isabella began the process – it is now out in the open (V, 1).
How should the Duke act?
Man is flesh and man is spirit – he goes wrong if, when placed in authority, he forgets the former and embraces the latter, in the belief that he is the sole repository of virtue.
The Duke forgives Angelo – only by the exercise of mercy can the law be rightly exercised in the world. This is vital for true justice to be done. It is not a question of treating men according to their deserts – in the eyes of God, no man is deserving. But God shows mercy to mankind, therefore God's deputies on earth should show mercy towards their fellow-men.
Mercy (the earthly equivalent of Divine Grace) widely exercised at the end of the play. It is not laxity – suffering of the protagonists was necessary to foster the right conditions; it simply takes account of the way men really are – steers a middle way between licence and legalism, both seen as destructive forces in the play. This is true justice.

2 Show how the title, *Measure for Measure*, fits the plot of the play.

3 What do the low-life scenes contribute to the play?

4 Do you find Isabella an admirable character? Define your attitude towards her.

5 Consider the view that *Measure for Measure* is an artistic failure.

6 Show how the tense antagonisms of the play's first half are subsequently woven into as close a texture of issues reconciled.

7 Do you consider that the reconciliation and harmony at the end of the play are contrived at the expense of the characters' plausibility?

8 How far is it possible to equate the Duke with Divine Providence?

9 Is it possible to consider Angelo as a tragic figure?

10 Discuss the theme 'know thyself' in *Measure for Measure.*

11 Show how Shakespeare uses imagery to exemplify the themes of the play.

12 Argue the case for or against forgiving Angelo in the light of his villainy in the play.

13 Do you agree with the view that the play falls into two disparate halves?

14 'The style of *Measure for Measure* is skilfully shaped to suit material that, by its very nature, offers little scope for lyricism or sustained flights of the imagination.' Discuss.

15 'More than our brother is our chastity.' Do you find that this remark alienates your sympathy from Isabella?

16 'A tedious, ludicrous busybody, who revels in planning out other people's lives.' Do you consider this to be a fair assessment of the Duke and his role in *Measure for Measure*?

17 What part is played by disguise in *Measure for Measure*?

18 Discuss the theme of 'appearance and reality' in *Measure for Measure.*

19 'Claudio is a character (one of the few) with whom we can readily identify in *Measure for Measure.*' Discuss.

20 What importance, if any, would you assign to Barnardine in the play?

21 In what sense might the play be termed a 'tragi-comedy'?

22 Discuss the character and importance of Pompey.

Further reading

The text:

The Arden Shakespeare: Measure for Measure, edited by J. W. Lever (Methuen 1967). The edition used in the preparation of these Notes.

The Signet Shakespeare: Measure for Measure, ed. S. Nagarajan (NAL)

Background to Shakespeare's plays:

The Elizabethan World Picture, E. M. W. Tillyard (Penguin, 1972)

Background to Shakespeare, M. M. Badawi (Macmillan, 1981)

Books on *Measure for Measure*:

Shakespeare: Measure for Measure, Nigel Alexander (Arnold, 1975)

Shakespeare's Measure for Measure, Mary Lascelles (Athlone Press, 1953)

Measure for Measure as Royal Entertainment, Josephine Bennett (Columbia University Press, 1966)

The Casebook on Measure for Measure, ed. Stead (Macmillan, 1971)

Useful material will be found in:

The Problem Plays of Shakespeare, Ernest Schanzer (Routledge, 1963)

Angel with Horns, A. P. Rossiter (Longman, 1961)

The Common Pursuit, F. R. Leavis (Penguin, 1962)

The Wheel of Fire, G. Wilson Knight (OUP, 1930)

Pan study aids Titles published in the Brodie's Notes series

W. H. Auden Selected Poetry

Jane Austen Emma Mansfield Park Northanger Abbey Persuasion Pride and Prejudice

Anthologies of Poetry Ten Twentieth Century Poets The Poet's Tale The Metaphysical Poets

Samuel Beckett Waiting for Godot

Arnold Bennett The Old Wives' Tale

William Blake Songs of Innocence and Experience

Robert Bolt A Man for All Seasons

Harold Brighouse Hobson's Choice

Charlotte Brontë Jane Eyre

Emily Brontë Wuthering Heights

Robert Browning Selected Poetry

John Bunyan The Pilgrim's Progress

Geoffrey Chaucer (parallel texts editions) The Franklin's Tale The Knight's Tale The Miller's Tale The Nun's Priest's Tale The Pardoner's Tale Prologue to the Canterbury Tales The Wife of Bath's Tale

Richard Church Over the Bridge

John Clare Selected Poetry and Prose

Samuel Taylor Coleridge Selected Poetry and Prose

Wilkie Collins The Woman in White

William Congreve The Way of the World

Joseph Conrad The Nigger of the Narcissus & Youth The Secret Agent

Charles Dickens Bleak House David Copperfield Dombey and Son Great Expectations Hard Times Little Dorrit Oliver Twist Our Mutual Friend A Tale of Two Cities

Gerald Durrell My Family and Other Animals

George Eliot Middlemarch The Mill on the Floss Silas Marner
T. S. Eliot Murder in the Cathedral Selected Poems

J. G. Farrell The Siege of Krishnapur

Henry Fielding Joseph Andrews

F. Scott Fitzgerald The Great Gatsby

E. M. Forster Howards End A Passage to India
Where Angels Fear to Tread

William Golding Lord of the Flies The Spire

Oliver Goldsmith Two Plays of Goldsmith: She Stoops to Conquer; The Good Natured Man

Graham Greene Brighton Rock The Power and the Glory
The Quiet American

Thom Gunn and Ted Hughes Selected Poems

Thomas Hardy Chosen Poems of Thomas Hardy
Far from the Madding Crowd Jude the Obscure
The Mayor of Casterbridge Return of the Native
Tess of the d'Urbervilles The Trumpet-Major

L. P. Hartley The Go-Between The Shrimp and the Anemone

Joseph Heller Catch-22

Ernest Hemingway For Whom the Bell Tolls
The Old Man and the Sea

Barry Hines A Kestrel for a Knave

Gerard Manley Hopkins Poetry and Prose of Gerard Manley Hopkins

Aldous Huxley Brave New World

Henry James Washington Square

Ben Jonson The Alchemist Volpone

James Joyce A Portrait of the Artist as a Young Man

John Keats Selected Poems and Letters of John Keats

Ken Kesey One Flew over the Cuckoo's Nest

Rudyard Kipling Kim

D. H. Lawrence The Rainbow Selected Tales Sons and Lovers

Harper Lee To Kill a Mockingbird

Laurie Lee As I Walked out One Midsummer Morning
Cider with Rosie

Thomas Mann Death in Venice & Tonio Kröger
Christopher Marlowe Doctor Faustus Edward the Second

W. Somerset Maugham Of Human Bondage

Gavin Maxwell Ring of Bright Water

Arthur Miller The Crucible Death of a Salesman

John Milton A Choice of Milton's Verse Comus and Samson Agonistes Paradise Lost I, II

Sean O'Casey Juno and the Paycock
The Shadow of a Gunman and the Plough and the Stars

George Orwell Animal Farm 1984

John Osborne Luther

Alexander Pope Selected Poetry

Siegfried Sassoon Memoirs of a Fox-Hunting Man

Peter Shaffer The Royal Hunt of the Sun

William Shakespeare Antony and Cleopatra As You Like It Coriolanus Hamlet Henry IV (Part I) Henry IV (Part II) Henry V Julius Caesar King Lear Love's Labour's Lost Macbeth Measure for Measure The Merchant of Venice A Midsummer Night's Dream Much Ado about Nothing Othello Richard II Richard III Romeo and Juliet The Sonnets The Taming of the Shrew The Tempest Twelfth Night The Winter's Tale

G. B. Shaw Androcles and the Lion Arms and the Man
Caesar and Cleopatra The Doctor's Dilemma Pygmalion Saint Joan

Richard Sheridan Plays of Sheridan: The Rivals; The Critic;
The School for Scandal

John Steinbeck The Grapes of Wrath Of Mice and Men & The Pearl

Tom Stoppard Rosencrantz and Guildenstern are Dead

J. M. Synge The Playboy of the Western World

Jonathan Swift Gulliver's Travels

Alfred Tennyson Selected Poetry

William Thackeray Vanity Fair

Flora Thompson Lark Rise to Candleford

Dylan Thomas Under Milk Wood

Anthony Trollope Barchester Towers

Mark Twain Huckleberry Finn

Keith Waterhouse Billy Liar
Evelyn Waugh Decline and Fall Scoop

H. G. Wells The History of Mr Polly

John Webster The White Devil

Oscar Wilde The Importance of Being Earnest

Virginia Woolf To the Lighthouse

William Wordsworth The Prelude (Books 1, 2)

John Wyndham The Chrysalids

W. B. Yeats Selected Poetry